# Hold the Bubble and Squeak

# Hold the Bubble and Squeak

✦

## A Run In with the Full English Breakfast

*Randy Rigler*

iUniverse, Inc.

New York  Lincoln  Shanghai

# Hold the Bubble and Squeak
## A Run In with the Full English Breakfast

Copyright © 2007 by Randal S. Rigler

iUniverse books may be ordered through booksellers or by contacting:

iUniverse
2021 Pine Lake Road, Suite 100
Lincoln, NE 68512
www.iuniverse.com
1-800-Authors (1-800-288-4677)

Because of the dynamic nature of the Internet, any Web addresses or links contained in this book may have changed since publication and may no longer be valid.

The views expressed in this work are solely those of the author and do not necessarily reflect the views of the publisher, and the publisher hereby disclaims any responsibility for them.

ISBN: 978-0-595-47803-3 (pbk)
ISBN: 978-0-595-60030-4 (ebk)

Printed in the United States of America

# Contents

# *Vacation*

I grew up on a dairy on the flatlands of west Texas. But I was not a flat-lander at heart. I frequently use that line as an explanation for any number of my shortcomings. What can I say was so intolerable about living there? I will go ahead and be trite; the landscape was baked by the sun, swept by the winds, and coated by the dust. To me it was dull and dreary, and I couldn't wait to get out of there. Life was made somewhat tolerable by the much anticipated summer trips the family would take to the cool mountains of southern New Mexico. It was, as the license plates claim, the land of enchantment. The nostril-cleansing smell of rain-wetted sage and pine was a break from the odor of a mucky cow lot. It was during those trips that I felt most at peace with the world and I am grateful to my parents for providing those opportunities each summer without fail.

When Georgia and I became parents we determined to provide the same experiences for our children. The double benefit we realized was seeing the world through their eyes as well as our own. As young parents with a tight budget, most of the first trips we took were long drives to visit friends or family. But as the kids grew older and our financial ability increased we would find ways to include visits to significant historical or geographical sites. My love of the family summer vacation continued.

In the summer of 2000, we decided a trip to Europe would be a real treat for everyone in the family. Kara, our oldest, would be graduating from the University of Washington in the spring of 2001. Chris would be finishing his second year at Bellevue Community College. Tim would be turning 14 and preparing for his freshman year of high school. And Georgia and I had maintained an appearance of sanity through all those years. It would be a graduation gift of sorts for all of us.

We had one year to prepare for the trip and discovered we would need it. Our initial plan was to spend two weeks in England and Germany, our lands of ancestry. As we considered some of the places we wanted to see in each country, with stops in between, we realized the time would be better spent in one country. We felt the language problem would be manageable in England. Georgia had been there for a school project, so she could be our guide. Everyone heartily agreed to plan on traveling the summer of 2001, the last week of June through the first week of July.

Looking back, we are glad we planned to go ahead and not wait for another year. It was pre-9/11 and the market, although it had slowed, had not yet taken its nosedive. I was able to stash away money each month for the trip. Everybody was given an assignment to help with the preparation. I looked into the flights. Georgia researched hotels and B&Bs. Kara asked some of her more-traveled instructors at school for recommendations on sites to see. Chris would lay out our routes for travel with the car. Tim was to roughly plan what we could do about meals.

To aid in our preparation, Georgia and I relied on the services provided by Rick Steves, *Europe Through the Back Door.* The office is located in nearby Edmonds and we spent several hours there over two or three days. We even saw Rick there once and he spoke with us, our first contact with celebrity on the trip. We had wanted to keep it all to a decent budget and by using the books and tapes made available by Rick Steves we trusted it could be done.

Every B&B that Georgia looked into proudly offered a Full English Breakfast as a prime benefit. We were happy because it appeared that at least one meal each day was already provided to us. Little did we know at the time what we were in for. Historically, the Full English is a monster of a meal. The variety of meats, puddings, vegetables, breads, eggs, and teas were not typical for the everyday English home, nor could we expect such a full fare, but the possibility of what was once the standard could make one's jaw drop, or more likely one's stomach. As it was we would have only access to the fried eggs, fried bacon, fried mushrooms, fried tomatoes, fried toast, and juice. Still, it sounded fun in theory. Like unwary Tokyo, we were about to meet the gastronomic Godzilla, the Full English Breakfast.

The time approached and things were falling into place. I booked the flights and Georgia made the reservations at the B&Bs. The kids went along with it and humored us. We were not at all worried about traveling together because it had always worked out for us. It was rather comforting knowing we would be together in this big adventure. We had our passports, a few pounds of cash to start out with, and we were ready to go. A friend drove us to the airport and we were on our way.

The following account is mostly true, or based on truth, or a flagrant concoction of fantasy and possibility. I hope the stated historical tidbits are true. A lot of compulsive, I do love history, research went into this that I wish I had before the trip. But most likely I would have driven the kids crazy with historic drivel before the trip was over. So here it is in print. Skip over it if you like.

Also, a friend read my first draft and stated it was ok, but maybe a bit boring. In an attempt at entertainment I played with some flights of fantasy at the start of most chapters. The concern of putting people off as a result kept haunting me. Then I remembered, as my friend had pointed out, I am no writer. The pressure is off and I can live down to my literary expectations. So carry on.

# DAY ONE: The Night That Never Was

The wide Atlantic took us hours to cross in a speeding jet. The narrow channel of water separating the islands currently known as the British Isles from the rest of the European continent has not prevented humans, as individuals and as groups, from making that crossing throughout the centuries. Some invaded, some raided, and most settled. Recorded history begins with the Roman invasion, subjugation, and colonization around the turn of the first century AD. For the Roman troops stationed there it was a harsh and often hostile frontier. When the troops were finally pulled back to defend Rome, no doubt most were glad to leave, but many had made roots and would stay.

With little more than what has been provided by Hollywood, I began my historical discovery of Britain. I had to wonder what it must have been like to serve overseas there. This could have been a typical blog picked up from one of the recruits.

◆　　◆　　◆

"Dear folks. So ends another day at the end of the world. I have been put on night watch for tonight and am not looking too forward to it. The other soldiers will be comfortable around the fire inside while I stand here in the dreary, mouldy, drafty air. Tell the kids back home to never listen to those recruiters. 'See the known world.' Indeed! Sadly enough I wanted to get away from home, sorry about that, and signed up. First they gave me a spear and sent me to Sicily for basic. Then I was called to this Zeus-forsaken island and now home never looked so good. Here the weather is so dreary and wet, the countryside so uninspiring, and the food so bland. Plus the locals haven't been too enthusiastic about our presence. What is their problem? We civilized them, liberated them, although from what I don't know. Now our leaders have stated that our mission has been accomplished and we can live in peace. Rome is safe. Well if that is so, then who keeps hacking up our patrols outside the walls?

As it is we have located, or maybe created, only one WMD (that would be a woman of mass destruction). Some queen of one of the local tribes feels she and her daughters were treated unfairly and rather roughly. The guys were just having a little fun. Besides, they are women; what do they expect? We are lonely men away from home, Roman men at that. And we were only following orders from higher up.

Last night a lot of campfires were seen surrounding the city and we are all a little nervous. Not all of our spies have returned. Those that did reported seeing an enormous gathering of people, frightful in appearance. They estimated it was in the thousands, men and women. I am afraid they are not here for trading, more likely collecting. Word is the women fight along with the men. And what I hear is they all fight mostly naked. That would sure be a sight to see, but I am afraid it might be the last I ever see. Can you picture one of these wild women, in a war chariot at that?"

◆     ◆     ◆

Here I stand staring at the bronzed Boudicca in her war chariot, she is clothed of course, out of English decency. Kara has just finished relating to us the story of the wild queen that sacked London. But I think my mind wandered a little off from her explanation, maybe way off. What was in those tablets Georgia gave us on the plane? They were intended to prevent jet lag and seemed to be working fine, until we landed. That was when the beneficial effects wore off, or were cancelled by reality.

Our long anticipated family vacation to England had started on Thursday around noon in Seattle and some 14 long, airborne hours later we landed at London's Gatwick airport early Friday morning. Eager, we exited the plane, hefting our Rick Steves life support units, matching black backpack/bags that we had marked with different colored pieces of ribbon, and approached the agent at the gate as a group, a small band of foreign invaders. He glanced quickly over my passport and without looking up asked, "So have you come to inflict a little pain?" He must have noticed my stated occupation—dentist.

"No, that is Mr. Rigler, not Ripper. But don't get me started on the oral condition I am dreading bearing witness to over here. They do say that was what sent old Uncle 'Jack The' over the edge."

That wasn't what I said. It was more like, "Huh?" I was already too jet-lagged to be much of a smart aleck.

"The trains are that way." He smiled kindly and sent us on through. Undoubtedly even sly terrorists couldn't have acted as pitiful as we must have been and appeared.

The train ride into town was too short for a nap. We rode silently, not yet sullenly. Soon the train disgorged us at Victoria Station, a combination train, bus, and subway terminal, as well as an indoor mall. Queues of people, no lines form, just queues, were rushing to trains and buses, refreshments, stores, or escalators. Since it was still early in the morning and we were newly arrived, I don't recall noticing the loitering homeless and pissing drunks that were impossible not to see on our subsequent passes through the station.

Upon exiting the station, we walked single file on the narrow sidewalk, all the while trying to stay on the proper side and out of the bustling street. We had been warned to look both ways when approaching a street because traffic would be coming from the direction opposite to what we were accustomed. And we truly wanted to 'meet the locals' under safer circumstances. The five of us puffing along with our matching black bags on our backs must have been a comical sight to behold. A sign around our necks proclaiming 'Tourist' would not have been necessary. Fortunately for us after walking in such a manner for only 2–3 blocks we were able to get off the main street. Then after wandering a few blocks down a quieter street we eventually began to wonder where the hell our B&B was. We weren't sure if we were going the right direction on even the right street. The block on which we thought it was located had a line of old three-story buildings that all looked alike.

We continued our search, finally found it, were buzzed in, and spoke with the woman behind the desk. In a heavy French accent she directed us to our rooms in the annex, a building one block back the way we came. Georgia and I had a room on the second floor and the kids were up in the attic on the fourth floor. After dumping our stuff we had our first planning conference in their room. What did we want to do first? Sleep! No, we couldn't do that. We had to force our bodies to pick up the new time schedule and forget they missed a night's rest. In that case we decided food would be a good second choice.

We were back on the street with only slightly less baggage. A couple of us carried backpacks and we all had strapped on our money belts under our clothing. We hiked to the bus station back on the main street to get to the café there. This station was where busses departed for other cities, unlike Victoria Station, which was a center for busses serving stops within the city of London. We discovered it didn't actually have a café, but rather a feeble mini-mart with a couple of small tables and a few chairs. The food we browsed over behind the glass doors confirmed our fears. Unappealing tuna sandwiches, prepared with corn, and a small selection of pathetic looking fruits dared us to just try. They were a good enough excuse for candy bars and juices.

On a fragile sugar high we started out for our first stop, Westminster Abbey. The pamphlet we consulted noted it was only a mile from Victoria Station, an easy walk. We figured we could handle that for our first trek out. We still managed to appear lost most of the time. Most often if we stood still and looked disoriented, which was easy to do, someone would come up to us and ask if we could use some assistance. I was impressed with the sincere British hospitality.

We arrived at the Abbey and the queue for entrance was not too long as yet. We were set for our first brush with history. It was time to realize the sites and buildings we would be seeing over the next few days had been standing for centuries. At the site of Westminster Abbey there has been a church standing for as far back as the seventh century AD. Although there is no evidence to confirm it, it has been suggested that Serbert, King of East Saxons, founded the first church in the early 600's. However, the first church of official record was erected by St. Dunstan around 960 AD. He had it built in honor of St. Peter and it was known as Westminster to distinguish it from the cathedral built in honor of St. Paul, the East Minster. Then in 1065, King Edward the Confessor built a new abbey in the Norman French style. In the mid-1200's, King Henry III had much of that one taken down and rebuilt in the then fashionable Gothic style. That is how it stands today.

Henry, Edward, and Serbert were all kings, but just who was this St. Dunstan? Born in the early 900's, this devoted cleric served as Abbot of Glastonbury, Bishop of London, and Archbishop of Canterbury. He also was a political advisor and negotiator for several of the English kings. He helped arrange a time of peace with the Danish invaders/settlers. Viking raids had eliminated monastic life; they especially preyed upon monasteries because of their riches. He reinstated a monastic presence in England. He was the most revered saint of England until Beckett.

Now the following tidbits concerning Dunstan may be on the urban-legend side, but he was also credited with grabbing the devil by the nose with a pair of smithing tongs. He also was said to have nailed a horseshoe to the devil's foot and removed it only after the devil promised to never enter a premises where a horseshoe is over the door. He thereby invented the lucky horseshoe.

Back to our entry into Westminster. After stepping inside and allowing our eyes to adjust to the dimmer lighting, we were struck by the quiet that the crowd inside held out of respect for all that was around them. We wanted to talk to each other, albeit quietly, because of what we were seeing. Soon after entering we especially desired to see a bathroom, or water closet, or toilet, or even the little symbols for a man or a woman. However the facilities would be marked, we weren't readily spotting them. An information person pointed them out.

This leads to some information I flushed out on the history of the toilet. The flushing toilet itself is a recent invention of only the past 150 years. Prior to that wastes made their way from private or public outhouses to the sewer drain or were merely tossed from a pot out into the street, from there to be washed into the sewer. As most large cities were on or very near a river, the sewage eventually made its way there. A London newspaper headline of 1859 proclaimed: "India Is In Revolt, and The Thames Stinks." Therefore, the advent of the flushing toilet and more responsible waste disposal made life in large cities more feasible.

Contrary to the popular legend, Thomas Crapper did not invent the toilet. Many had worked on the problem, even Leonardo de Vinci had drawn plans for one, but like his helicopter it wasn't to be a reality until centuries later. After the flushing toilet became a household item, the early manufacturers would place their name on a bowl as a form of marketing. Evidently a lot of Crappers were seen and the name stuck. Prior to the crapper, the monks of Westminster referred to the hole in the floor as the 'necessarium' and chances were it could be located by smell alone.

Speaking of monks and odor, Westminster was originally operated by monks of the Benedictine order. This strict order originated in France. They wore black habits, hence called Blackfriars, and bathed only four times per year. It wasn't just a single guy thing. To the Christians of that day Rome was a symbol of worldliness and evil, sort of an early USA. Cleanliness, particularly bathing, was an important part of

Roman life. Therefore, cleanliness was not next to godliness and was discouraged. In the words of St. Benedict himself, "to those that are well, especially for the young, bathing shall seldom be permitted." Rome and the utilities companies have prevailed.

The Benedictine involvement itself with Westminster was ended in 1540, when Henry VIII dissolved the monastery. At that time the Abbey was then designated as a 'Royal Peculiar,' an appropriate combination of words, which meant it was governed directly by the monarchy, God's chosen, and not by any particular religious order.

As with any proper church, whether Saxon, Norman, Gothic, or Peculiar, the layout is the shape of a cross. All along the cross tour route that we followed there were diversions into memorial side chambers and offshoots; it was a maze of over three thousand tombs and dedications. The revered and honored of England are buried there. Several kings, Edwards and Henrys, and queens, Marys and Elizabeths, are interred there. Numerous other lords and ladies, saints and poets, distinguished people all, were in stone chambers above the floor or below. Now that I think of it, it would be a great setting for a 'Dawn of the Dead' horror movie scene. Hands would crash from the sides of stone coffins and up from tombs in the floor. The crowd of screaming tourists would move in a mad rush for the door. The likes of Shakespeare and Chaucer would be attacking a group of high school English Lit students. Out of respect it is just as well such a scene has not been attempted, at least not that I am aware of. Besides, Churchill, for one, was scary enough in real life. For the time we were there the dead slept, honored and underfoot.

We had not been there long before the crowds began to pick up, creating bottlenecks at various entryways. We all got separated and I was soon tired of walking this mausoleum. We were each beginning to manifest our own symptoms of jet lag, the most common being irritability. We got back together and agreed on at least one thing, we needed food. We were done with Westminster Abbey.

Big Ben was only a bit farther down the street and we all grumpily agreed we wanted to at least see it. The Parliament Building was on our way. It is a large government building on the bank of the Thames. We looked at it and then continued on to Westminster Bridge. The kids posed there for a couple of shots with Big Ben in the background and we were ready to head back to our B&B.

Across the street from where we took our pictures of Big Ben was the statue of Queen Boudicca. This was where I had pondered the fate of the Roman recruit at the beginning of this chapter. Kara, the recent history grad, related the story of Boudicca. She was queen of the Iceni, one of the Celtic tribes, the native inhabitants of England prior to the arrival of the Romans, and the later Saxons, Angles, Danes, and Normans. The Roman occupiers had a firm, although begrudged, hold on the lands. The husband of Boudicca, the king, had died leaving her and her two daughters half of his estate and wealth. Since this tribe, along with others, had sworn subservience to the Roman Emperor, the Roman governor of England assumed he deserved all the inheritance and took offence. In his flawed judgment he thought it would be best to make of her an example. She was imprisoned and flogged, and her daughters were beaten and raped. She was enraged and upon her release she gathered an army that reportedly numbered almost 100,000. Now, exaggeration of battle numbers has always been a common practice. However, since the local Roman general and his legion were busy fighting druids in northern Wales, the remaining garrisons were badly outnumbered. In addition, Celtic women fought along with and equaled their men in battle. The Romans were frustrated when faced with men and women, many of both naked and painted, screaming and singing madly as they charged in. Boudicca sacked and burned the settlement of Londonium and several others before finally being defeated in a blaze of glory as the Roman legion hurried back. This story confirmed our hopes that four years of college tuition payments were not in vain; that and it taught us never to cross a Celtic warrioress.

As we turned from Queen Boudicca, someone mentioned seeing the Queen Elizabeth II Conference Centre nearby and at that suggestion someone else snapped. No doubt about it, we needed food—immediately. What we quickly discovered was English eating establishments were not open during the hours to which we were accustomed at home. Door after door we passed posted the hours open as 11:00 to 1:00 or 2:00, and then open again no earlier than 6:00, and usually 7:00. We were in need at the moment and it was only 5:00. Our meals from the bus terminal that morning were long gone. We were all coming down fast. Kara threatened to sit down on the walkway right where we stood and wait for the confounded restaurant to open. A quick glance at our map of London showed no Shite Creek, but we were definitely up it and no paddles would be available for another hour or two.

Up and down the streets we trudged, our feet tired and hungry. At one point we entered what we thought was a pub, Rick Steves had recommended trying one, and learned there were pubs and there were bars. We had entered a bar and Tim, being 14 years old, was not welcome. We had to wonder what the hell hungry Londoners did between 2:00 and 6:00 other than go to a bar. We were in a real crisis.

At last we found a Chinese restaurant that was open. The food was not remarkable, but we had plates in front of us. During the meal Chris discovered a plastic chopstick was no substitute for a knife. A chunk of sweet-and-sour pork was too tough and his attempt to cut it with a chopstick resulted in half the utensil flying across the quiet room with a loud snap. After a hearty laugh and with food in our stomachs, our tension was finally broken, too.

At the end of the meal we had to reach some conclusion on tipping while in England. At home, since Kara had done time as a restaurant server, we generally tipped around 20%. Our travel books had recommended 5% and we thought that was grossly inadequate. We compromised at 10%. After all, we had ruined one plastic chopstick. At the time we did not realize a gratuity had already been added to our bill. It was no wonder the waiter kept bowing and thanking us as we left.

Once we were fed, we willed our lead feet to carry us back to our B&B. Sure it was early, only just after 6:00, but at the moment we were literally the walking dead. We needed sleep. The kids clomped upstairs to their room and Georgia and I settled into ours. This was when I finally took stock of our rooms. The kids' was really a small attic room, complete with sloping ceiling on the far side of the room. Our room was different. First, the ceiling was at least ten feet high. We had only one bed, but it mostly filled the room, allowing merely two to three feet of clearance around it. The water closet was off to the side and the door to it couldn't open all the way because of the bed. Nevertheless, in our exhausted state it would do quite well.

After getting ready for bed I located the remote required for operating the TV that was perched high atop the wardrobe at the foot of the bed. I found only five channels, and two of those were the same one. Cable surfing would be abbreviated. I turned it off, closed my eyes, and was immediately gone. Yet it seemed only minutes later that Georgia wakened me. "Randy, wake up. My watch says 7:30 and I don't know if it is AM or PM." She had already gotten up, showered, and dressed. The outside lighting was no help because it was at that stage where one could assume it was early morning or early evening either way. Truly, if it was AM, then we all needed to get up and get ready for the day. I just couldn't help feeling I had only slept a few minutes. I searched for the remote and she ran upstairs to see if the kids had any way of knowing whether it was AM or PM. I finally made sense of the telly and was pretty sure it was still PM. Georgia came back to the room and said the kids had assured her it was evening as they sleepily checked Tim's watch.

So ended our first day in England. At least we could get back to sleep and catch up on much needed rest. It was a good thing we didn't get all dressed up and go over to the dining room for our anticipated Full English Breakfast. The B&B staffers, had there been any there, would surely have wondered about this odd American family. Since we were among the English, they would have most likely looked at each other with a knowing look, corrected us politely, offer an apology that it wasn't morning, and then promptly retreat to the back room chuckling.

# DAY TWO: Whatever Happened to Mithra?

At the end of the first night we made a hasty plan for the goals of the next day. We definitely wanted to see the Tower of London, a must-see for any tourist in London. As tired as we were it was all we could to just to make that decision. As I lay on the bed waiting for sleep, I glanced over the pamphlet for the Tower and read bits of its centuries of intrigue and history. I did not read much; my eyes clanged shut like a heavy wooden door to a tower keep. Dreams of gibbets danced in my head.

◆　　　◆　　　◆

"We will just see who can produce the sonnet which most pleases His Majesty. I do hope that maid carried through with my request. I gave her enough of the powder to kill a small army. I eased her suspicions by telling her it possessed aphrodisiacal properties. Her eyes were lit with a lusty flame at that revelation. Her desire for Sir Thomas only makes this scheme of mine more workable. Undoubtedly she will try to slip him some at the soonest opportune moment in anticipation of a romantic tryst with that pompous fool.

"I say, he sure has been in that loo for a long time. Ha! I hope there is not some poor soul lurking about the walls tonight. With his fat arse hanging out over the wall and the poison working its purging throes, it would be very unfortunate to be near the drop. I do wonder which morsel of the meal she placed the powder in. He consumed everything in sight so greedily that she could not have put it in any wrong portion.

It is just as well he refuses any company when his creative urges overtake him, and when he overtakes his venison.

"Then I am sure she will partake of a portion herself, thus eliminating any connection with myself in what will appear to be a tragic case of suicide between two lovers. But now that I think on it, she may not feel she has any need herself for a lover's potion. She already has an enormous lust for Sir Thomas. For that matter, she has an enormous lust for almost any man. I only barely escaped her amorous advances. A dreadfully frightening situation it was. I will be only too glad to once and for all be rid of her as well as that usurper to my rightful place as King's Poet.

"From the sounds issuing from the loo I can only assume the poison is having its effect on his body. But such travails? What if she is so sure of her fulfilling her passions that she has administered the entire dose to him? Oh dear, this may prove to be a stickier situation than I had hoped. And what is that sound, that buzzing as of a hive of angry bees?

◆    ◆    ◆

That buzzing was nothing more than the alarm telling me it was 7:30, time to get up. Only one day in the land of courtly intrigue had already fed strange images into my dreams. My eyes were still groggy from the lingering jet lag, but definitely better than 7:30 the night before. And the much anticipated encounter with the promised Full English Breakfast, FEB, was only minutes away. A shower and a shave and I would be all set.

Bathroom, toilet, water closet, 'necessarium', surely they are all the same. Right away the shower presented the first challenge. It seemed simple enough, a showerhead attached to a flexible metal hose. Turning the single knob engaged the water. It should have been straightforward enough, just turn the knob counterclockwise and the water gets hotter. I turned and turned the thing, but passed through warm, only extremely briefly, and never twice in the same spot. The knob finally fell off from undoubtedly excessive turning. I showered with the least cold compromise I could find.

The next challenge was operating the hairdryer. Before leaving we had made sure the one we took with us had a switch to accommodate the change from 110V to 220V. What we had not known was that the outlets themselves were different; a circular, three-pronged set-up instead of the familiar two vertical slits. Surely we could have found an adapter, but never tried hard enough. Since there would be no dryer time in the mornings that meant only less time spent each morning while a FEB was waiting.

Perhaps I was a little too excited about the upcoming meal, which is not really a recommendation when in England. We had noted each B&B we booked listed a 'Full English Breakfast' as a special feature and assumed it had to be something noteworthy. Websites I have visited since our trip have declared the FEB to be dead, except as offered to tourists in hotels and B&Bs. As it died I am sure it took many consumers with it. In its better days it would strain a table as well as a body. Such would be the spread: devilled kidneys, Scotch kippers, honey pancakes, black pudding, kedgeree, coiled wild boar sausage, farm smoked bacon, wholemeal toast, freshly churned butter, fruit preserves, free-range duck and chicken eggs, bubble and squeak, sautéed field mushrooms, grilled tomatoes, grapefruit, ground coffee, Darjeeling tea in a china pot, and freshly squeezed orange juice. Alas, what was offered to us was but a trifle in comparison. Still, I was glad to forego the devilled kidneys, the bubble and squeak (leftover veggies from dinner—they bubble and squeak when cooking), kedgeree (flaked fish with boiled rice), and especially black pudding (pig's blood, suet, bread, barley, oatmeal).

So it was with innocent anticipation that we walked into the breakfast room and started with coffee and juices. A table set with cereals and fruits tempted us a little, but we held off. Then the plates were set before us, each covered with a large serving of fried eggs, fried mushrooms, fried ham slices (they called it bacon), fried toast (why?), steamed or fried tomato chunks, beans, sausage, and dry toast. Seems a common ingredient of a FEB was fat, from frying. Fortunately for us we got out of the country before our arteries shut down or our bowels clogged up. To this day we rarely eat eggs at home any more, and beans for breakfast are entirely out of the question.

With grease-laden stomachs we hit the street. Our money belts, as recommended by and purchased from Rick Steves, needed filling, too. Each was a lightweight, zippered, cloth pouch with a thin strap to attach it around the waist. Although they were definitely more secure than a pants pocket or purse, I really disliked walking to a public ATM and reaching down into the front of my pants. Once accomplished as discreetly as possible, we proceeded to Victoria Station and purchased two-day passes to use the Tube, the underground trains.

The Tube was a fun experience. It didn't take too long to figure out the platforms and appropriate stops, and by using it we could easily reach most of our destinations. What we really enjoyed was the recorded message that would play as a train approached a stop. A dry, electronic voice said, "Mind the gap," in a certain way that caused us to giggle each time we heard it. It became our catchphrase for London. Tim searched several shops until he finally found a 'Mind the Gap' T-shirt and we simply had to buy it. Fortunately we decided against buying matching shirts for all of us.

The Tube took us past several stops: Westminster, Temple, Black-friars, to our first destination of the day, the Tower of London. Approaching from our stop we could see the Tower takes up 5–6 city blocks. It isn't a single structure, but a number of buildings and towers, all built at different times. The central building, the White Tower, was the original tower, or castle, and was built by William, the Duke of Normandy around 1078 AD. For several centuries it served as both a residence for the royal family and as the center of government. Over time succeeding monarchs built other towers and buildings until the family and government were eventually relocated.

As was noted in the guide we picked up at the entrance, near the beginning of the tour route was the Bloody Tower and its gruesome name conjured up in our minds scenes of torture, so we made straight for it. As it was, there were no instruments of torture or execution on display here, only chambers of confinement. Presumably the name originated as the result of the disappearance and murder of two young princes on the premises in 1485. One had been smothered with a pillow and the other, up until that time the future king, was stabbed to death. Another departure of note was a Sir Thomas Overby, a poet and courtier. His food had been poisoned and it is said he ingested enough to kill 20 men, a forerunner to the FEB.

Not all housed here received such harsh treatment. The tower also served as a quarters for prisoners of note. One such was Sir Walter Raleigh. The residence was displayed as it was probably furnished during his lengthy stay and it looked as if his family stayed there at times, too. It had a large bed, a modest desk, and several bookcases. During his stay he conducted numerous scientific experiments, thereby developing the method for distilling fresh water from salt water. He also wrote a book, *The History of the World,* which was published while he was there. The book's notoriety would have gotten to his head if only he hadn't parted with it, his head, after 13 years in the tower.

I had to pause to consider if Sir Walter Raleigh would mean anything to the kids. He received some mention in history classes of my day and he was seen all around on cans of tobacco, but what about today? Raleigh, 1554–1618, was well known as a writer, poet, courtier, explorer, and military leader. As a result of his trips to the new world he is said to be the first to have brought back and planted potatoes in Ireland. It is also thought he introduced the smoking of tobacco to England. One day while he was out in his garden with his pipe, his servant doused him with a bucket of water; he thought his master was on fire. Raleigh named the colony he started in the new world Virginia, in honor of the virgin queen, Elizabeth I. That was where there may have been a little fire. He was a favorite of hers and even taught her to smoke. Her attention to him made enemies for him in the court. After the death of Queen Elizabeth in 1603, the new King James was not as enamored with him. Raleigh was implicated, most likely unjustly, in a plot to overthrow the king and was then imprisoned. After 13 years of imprisonment he was beheaded and his head was presented to his wife. She had it embalmed and is said to have kept it with her always. She would often ask her visitors if they wanted to see Sir Walter. Thankfully, she had no interest in ventriloquism. She was not a candidate for a second marriage.

Following the Bloody Tower was a walk-through of the Medieval Palace, restored as it might have appeared in the 13$^{th}$ century. Evidently it was in the process of being remodeled because it was very sparse looking, not at all how it would have been when King Edward I (of Braveheart fame) resided there. After the Palace we walked along the wall overlooking Traitor's Gate, through which prisoners were brought in to the Tower, usually only a one-time event. Following the wall walk we noted the Lanthorn Tower, Cradle Tower, Well Tower, Salt Tower, and Develin Tower. That was a hell of a lot of towers, all within a few feet of each other. Most often they were used to hold prisoners.

Near the Wardrobe Tower (no Spare Oom Tower?) we paused by the fragment of Roman wall standing on the green. The White Tower had been built where Claudius had previously erected a Roman fort. At the moment this segment of Roman wall was the territory of the Tower Ravens. This was not a new punk group out of London, but a group of ravens that are maintained on the site. A posted sign warned of their tendency to bite viciously if approached. Only the Tower Raven Master, high level, could manage them. His duty was to feed and care for them, each night putting them to bed, or cage, or nest, or roost, or whatever. His nightly tradition sounded as honored as that of the changing guards at the palace. Each evening when the Raven Master approaches, the leader of the unkindness (in England a group of ravens is known as an 'unkindness' rather than as a 'murder', as crows are known) swoops down in front of the Raven Master and assumes an aggressive posture; wings spread open, neck feathers ruffed, and with a raucous cawing. The current Raven Master admits this behavior was unsettling the first time he faced it, but at that time he decided to respond in a like manner. So each time now, he squats down, cocks his arms, and caws back at the raven. Thus satisfied, the ravens all submit and will continue to do so as long as the Raven Master is bigger than they are.

One might ask why ravens, wings clipped to prevent escape, are maintained on the Tower grounds. Legend is there is an old superstition that states if there is ever a time when there are no ravens at the Tower, then the Tower will fall and so will the British Commonwealth. King Charles II was responsible for the decree stating at all times there will be six ravens kept at the Tower. Originally the royal observatory was located in a dome on the White Tower. On one occasion the Royal Astronomical Observator went to peer out the telescope, no doubt at the window in the building next door, and was enraged to find the lens covered with bird crap. He complained to the King and the birds were ordered executed, summarily. One of the King's advisors alerted him of the raven superstition. Since the King had just returned the monarchy to the throne, following a bloody civil war, he decided to take no chances and commuted their sentence. The birds stayed, but the observatory was moved to Greenwich. At the current time the ravens have been moved indoors to the safety of cages. Bird flu is not going to take down the English government.

The Rick Steves book had advised us to get to the Crown Jewel exhibit early on to avoid the inevitable lengthy queues. We were early and there was not much of a queue yet to speak of, but there was a steady flow of people passing through the display. It was a one-way stream that began with rooms and murals relating the history of the nation and its rulers from early times on. I do hope we will be forgiven our speed-reading and speed-listening; we were there to see the jewels. At the entry to the jewel room the flow slowed. We next had to step on to a moving walkway to be carried, buffet style, past the glass-encased crowns, scepters, jewels, baubles, spoons, etc. I found it impressive, but not breathtaking. It is interesting to note the majority of the current items were of 17<sup>th</sup> century workmanship. During the civil war of the mid-1600's the royal items of that time were taken and melted or destroyed. The rebels were far too shortsighted to realize the economic gain from the tourist potential of the originals.

The controlled flow past the jewels must have been an effort to curtail any funny business with them. Historically, there was one attempt to steal the Crown Jewels that was very nearly pulled off. Before being housed where they currently are, they were kept in the Martin Tower, under the watchful eye of the Keeper of the Jewels. At the time of the event the Keeper was a man named Edwards. A Sir Thomas Blood, in the guise of a clergyman, befriended the Keeper, even proposing a marriage between his 'nephew' and the daughter of Edwards. Blood brought his nephew and a friend to make the arrangements one evening. While there he asked if he could be granted just a little peek at the jewels. When Edwards opened the door the hoodlums attacked him, beating him viciously, and then stuffed what they could carry into their clothing. The timely return of Edwards' son caused the thieves to flee and the alarm was raised. The three were caught and brought before the king, Charles II, Raven Pardoner. The king said it had been a very bold and gallant attempt and therewith pardoned Blood and even granted him a pension. Keeper Edwards was given 200 pounds, but for unrelated reasons was forced to sell it off at half price and died of his incurred injuries shortly after.

To finish our tour of the Tower of London we entered the White Tower. This was the original building of the complex. After the royal family and government moved elsewhere it became an armoury and eventually a museum by the 17<sup>th</sup> century. The tour took us up and down stairs to see the chapel, the assembly room, and various rooms of weapons, armour, and heraldry. A small side trip gave us a memorable look through the hole in the loo to the drop zone below. This was a small chamber that jutted out from the exterior wall of the castle, a two-seater. Back on the tour was a room that contained life-sized duplications of some of the horses of many of the kings. An adjoining room had displays of suits of armour worn by the kings. Among them were three suits made for Henry VIII. At first I thought only two of the suits were his and the third was for his horse. Apparently in his later years his girth had become considerable.

The bottom floor of the White Tower housed a number of cannons and mortars, too heavy for upper floors. It also had the gift shop. It was our first gift shop; we were interested and tempted. Tim succumbed and bought a working paper model of an executioner and his client. Crank the lever, his axe goes down, and the victim's head drops off. Cute? A large portion of the Tower's fame is due to the many executions performed there, so perhaps it was an appropriate remembrance. All in all, the Tower of London was quite interesting, but the time had come to move on.

Rick Steves had recommended missing the nearby London Dungeon, calling it nothing of historical significance and merely a tourist trap. With that in mind, we crossed the Tower Bridge and found our way down the side streets to the entrance. It had all the commercial haunted house effects: smelly, fake mists swirling around the floor, black lights, moving skeletons and corpses, various screams and moans from within. That was all while the queue snaked to the ticket window. After purchasing tickets and as we approached the doors we had to pause while a family ahead of us posed for a picture of the kids holding axes and cleavers over the parents' heads. The chance was offered every party upon entrance and the pictures would be available for purchase at the end of the tour. Tainted minds. We passed on the offer.

The first segment was a historical walk-through of barbaric (unlike our 'civilized') methods of torture and death, accounts of gruesome disasters and infamous celebrities, and scenes of the darker side of historic London life. Bodies were hanging on hooks as rats scampered over them, William Wallace's head perched on a pike on London

Bridge, and an archbishop being assassinated by certain subjects more loyal to the king than the church.

A lovely part of the exhibit was a brief boat ride through the sewers of London. First we had to stand waiting for thirty minutes to get on and once on it was a short, smelly ride, but it still beat Disney's 'Small World' ride hands down. After disembarking we were treated to the Jack the Ripper show. This 19th century serial killer was really quite a gruesome fellow and the Dungeon capitalized on it with glee. Accordingly, his identity is still not known, but the theories range all the way from a member of the royal family to even an American surgeon, or dentist just as likely.

To escape the Dungeon we had to make a break through the great London fire of 1666. Our group of spectators was hurried along a dimly lit, narrowing hallway as lights and sounds simulated the roaring conflagration. Near the end of the hallway an exhibition worker, dressed in black so as to be hard to see, was obscurely posted head-level to one side of our mad rush and was intermittently squirting passers-by with small jets of water. Chris and Tim spotted him ahead of time and considered alerting the rest of us. Actually, they were watching to see if we got squirted, but somehow we avoided it. Exiting the Dungeon, we stopped for a bite in the Blood & Guts Café. Later in the trip when in York and Edinburgh we noted that the Dungeon was a chain and properly avoided any further contact, finally true to Rick Steves' recommendation.

There was still daylight left for us to explore; we crossed the River Thames on the London Bridge and made for St. Paul's Cathedral. Along the way we searched for a Roman temple to Mithra that was noted on our city map. We were surrounded by skyscrapers; temples to manna, but for all our looking could not spot Mithra's. St. Paul's, however, with its towering dome, was impossible to miss. Upon arriving and locating the front door we learned a more extensive tour of the underground crypt and of the Dome would not be available due to construction. That was too bad. An interesting feature of the Dome is that at a certain point on the way to the top is a section known as the Whispering Wall, where a whisper spoken against one wall is heard at the wall on the opposite side, 112 feet away. For the time we had there Georgia, Kara, and I sat to listen to a service that was in progress, while Chris and Tim went outside to wait on the steps. It was mostly choral music, but just to realize we were witnessing a service in St. Paul's Cathedral was a thrill. At the conclusion of the service we walked underneath the magnificent Dome to gaze up into it. At the same time ushers were firmly, but politely trying to get everyone to leave. It was closing time, but many tourists continued to mill about obliviously.

St. Paul's Cathedral is considered to be the spiritual center of the city of London, much like Seattle's Kingdome. The current structure is a relatively new building, from the late 17$^{th}$ century. The first church was established on the site by King Ethelbert and destroyed by a fire not many years later. It was rebuilt by St. Erkenwald, the London Bishop, in 675–85. Vikings leveled that one in 962. The building known as Old St. Paul's was built by the Normans on a grand scale beginning in the late 11$^{th}$ century and taking nearly 200 years to complete. This one suffered under neglect and decay after a few centuries, and more so during the Puritan revolutions. It was finally destroyed in the fire of 1666.

This is as good a place as any to expand a little on two events of the 1600's, which have been already alluded to: the Puritan Revolution and the London fire of 1666, both acts of a god of some sort. I tried to cram the English Civil War down in to one page, an offense to historians. Let me see if I can make it even briefer. An over-ambitious king, people suffering from heavy taxation to support wars, the Protestant Reformation, religion and rule. Putting it that way kind of scares me. King Charles I and the monarchy were overthrown by the armies of the Protestant Roundheads led by Oliver Cromwell. A Commonwealth, overseen by a Protectorate, was established. It lasted a brief while, but with the return of the monarchy, King Charles II, the Parliament was strengthened and the powers of the king diminished. During the Protestant rule symbols of the monarchy were destroyed and Catholic buildings, monasteries and cathedrals, were dismantled. An uneasy peace remains between Protestant and Catholic.

Just for fun I have to mention two tenets of the Anglican faith of the time that I liked simply because of their odd names. Free Will With Partial Depravity and Universal Atonement, But Only for Believers.

The other event, the London fire of 1666, is much simpler. A bakery caught fire and 80% of London burned to the ground. Much of what we know of the fire comes from the diary of Samuel Pepys, who observed it safely from the other side of the Thames River. Still, just to be safe, he buried his wine and Parmesan for protection. It was fortunate that only eight lives were lost. But St. Paul's was one of the buildings lost. As a side note, in 1986 the Baker's Company officially issued an apology for the fire.

Charles II, newly returned to the throne, commissioned the architect Christopher Wren to plan the repairs to the fire. Initially Wren was prepared to rebuild the entire city, with wide streets and more open spaces to make another such fire less possible. Charles thought his plan too costly, remembering the people's pockets were close to their rebellious souls, and wanted Wren to rebuild only the churches. St. Paul's was completed in 33 years, a remarkable feat at the time and is undeniably a masterpiece of architecture design. Within the building most of the tombs have a specific, elaborate commemoration to the person buried there. The tomb of Christopher Wren has just these words at the foot: "If you seek his memorial, look about you."

We left St. Paul's and went for the nearest tube station. We were walking back on the same street we had taken to St. Paul's earlier, only on the other side of the street. We could have stumbled on the temple to Mithra; actually we did stumble over it. There is nothing of it remaining above ground level and it is in a small space in front of a tall office building. During construction of the building the ancient foundation had been discovered, unearthed, and moved to its new location.

In the days of Roman rule the temple to Mithra would not have been so difficult to locate. The Mithraic cult, with probable roots in Persia, had a wide following amongst the soldiers of the Roman army. Its decline followed the decline of Rome and the rise of the new Christian religion. In fact, the early Christian cult was annoyed by the competition Mithra offered. But it is thought the Christians did borrow one item—the cross-shaped building of worship. Obviously Mithra would not appeal to the masses today because it was predominantly male oriented and stressed advancement on the basis of deeds of strength and valor. Or would it?

A quick ride on the Tube brought us back to our neighborhood and we stopped at the pub just across the street from our B&B. Rick Steves' book and other guides to the UK had encouraged a try at the pubs. Inside we found our own way to the dark and smoky room at the back and coaxed the waitress to come for our orders. The service and the food were both very unremarkable. At least we could say we tried a pub, but we did not feel inclined to try any more.

That night we slept very well, at least Georgia and I did. The kids had a laugh session they told us about the next day. While they were watching some lame movie, Chris began making farting sounds with the back of his knee, such talent. Kara and Tim made their own attempts to copy him and finally Tim had to settle for the standard armpit. In the process they laughed themselves nearly into convulsions. The next morning when they told us about it over breakfast they approached that hysterical condition again and years later when they talk about it tears come to their eyes. I guess you had to be there to fully appreciate it. The environment and fatigue level must have been just right and a stress breaker needed. Good they knew what to do.

# DAY THREE: Our Farewell to London

Picture swirling London fog, the clanking sounds of passing trains in the Tube, and distant voices. Imagine that somewhere in the dark underground of London there is a pub where denizens from previous centuries gather to moan over a pint of spirits. The 'Ghost Tour' guides don't have record of it and Rick Steves hasn't found it yet. Suppose we could witness one such meeting of two souls.

◆　　◆　　◆

"Egad man, you married a baby." He took a deep drink and wiped his bearded mouth with a flourish. The Bard of Avalon knew how to use a flourish.

His companion sat stiffly and took a stately sip. In his lifetime he was revered by thousands as a deity. He was.... Tut. "We had both seen only twelve years. I had no right to judge her immaturity. It was easier in your day. Marriage ages were generally much better, at least by a year or more."

"As vexing as a marriage between man and woman can be, it pales in comparison to the marriage between church and state. The body of religious fervor can be a frigid and shrewish bride."

"True. It was different at my time. As pharaoh I was god and king on earth."

"So thought, or at least wished, many of our kings. The Puritan Roundheads showed them otherwise."

"These Puritans you speak of, did they not teach of peace and brotherly love? And if their battle was with the ruling monarchy, then were you not safe? You had no royal blood."

"Alas, I was an actor, and a writer, and as such was as the anti-Christ in the eyes of the Puritans. Not a brick wall fell or fire was started that we were not given the blame for it. Even the plague was laid at our feet. We were truly the first bio-terrorists, to use an uncouth term of the current days."

"Ah yes, the current days. In these times my name is more often associated with a curse. Not the legacy I had hoped for."

"True. The entertainment industry of the twentieth century has had a field day with that one. You struck fear in their hearts then. That was respect at least."

"Respect? Do you think my meeting with Costello and the Abbott showed any respect?"

"Perhaps I understand. Leo dashed any hopes I had for my Romeo."

In the moment of silence that follows, they both stare into their mugs, possibly in their minds viewing scenes from their lives. Or maybe viewing something else. A smile begins to form on the Bard's mouth.

"I say. Did you ever see that Steve Martin bit on you?"

The Pharaonic eyes narrow and his lips tighten. "I was not 'born in Babylonia'." Then a twinkle shows in his eyes. "But I can totally 'do the Egyptian'."

The Bard spews his drink with a cough and they both burst into loud laughter.

◆    ◆    ◆

We were all in the dining room for our second FEB. We attempted some modifications. Scrambled eggs were only a slight improvement. The kids started passing some of their meals down to me. It was more than I needed, but I had already paid for them. Somebody better eat them.

On our third day in England we planned to finish London up with visits to the Globe Theatre, All-Hallows Church, and the British Museum. We were gluttons for punishment, trying to cram in some sights that really deserved more time than we could give them.

By then we had the tube down pretty well. Arriving at the Globe early on we got into one of the first tours of the morning. The current building is a recent reconstruction of what the original was in its time. It is roughly circular in shape, providing a ring around the stage. The wooden benches of the outer ring were under the roof, providing the more well to do with a degree of comfort during a show. It was no better than the current bleachers seating at a high school football stadium, but it beat the central area. There the rest of the playgoers would stand at the mercy of whatever weather was occurring. One benefit of the central area was those in front were right at the foot of the stage, providing ample opportunity for heckling and interacting with those on stage. It would have been an ideal stand-up comic setting, but a virtual dream for Gallagher and his smashing melons.

The Protestant Reformation had taken a firm hold as Europe underwent the Renaissance during the 16th and 17th centuries. An extreme form of the Reformation was found in the rise of Puritanism. Zealous piety was a trademark of the clergy and spokesmen, as opposed to what was generally seen as the sinful excesses and indulgences on the part of the monarchy. Dancing, as well as anything else enjoyable, was banished and churches even had their organs removed (ouch!). Theatre held a special place of contempt because, for one thing, it competed with the pulpit for the attention of the people, even daring so much as to hold plays on Sundays and holy days. In addition, the topics presented and the lines uttered by the actors were considered to be full of lewdness and irreverence. Since the majority of the performers were men, the role of a woman in a play was most often done by a man dressed in woman's clothing. Actors were looked on as no better than harlots, producing no tangible good for society, but living by beguiling the poor of their money. The righteous considered the occurrence of any accident or disaster as proof of God's displeasure with theatre. The plague, which ravaged Europe at intervals throughout the middle ages, was an obvious example. The logic used was simple: plagues are the result of sin, sin is caused by plays, therefore, plays caused plague. Plague appearances were cyclical and when an outbreak would manifest itself the actors in a town would be run out and refused entrance.

It was only the support theatre got from Elizabeth and the lordly court that allowed it to survive. However, as a result of that connection, theatre was an early casualty in the war between the 'catholic' monarchy and the puritan population. After the protestant victory in the Civil War, theatre was effectively banned. The Globe was torn down for housing. But the Puritan fervor waned, the monarchy returned, and theatre and the arts returned with a vengeance, triple the lasciviousness. The Puritans then sought to regain their way in the new world. So the new world colonies were settled by hopeful Puritans, that and by convicts the government wished to clear from their jails. Puritans and convicts, the two party system was established. Ah well, time to close the curtains on our visit to the Globe Theatre.

The next stop was the All-Hallows Church. The main reason the kids wanted to go there was the name. It just sounded kind of 'halloweenish', had to be spooky. A little preview informed us an underground chamber contained ancient Roman artifacts. The first church on the site was built in AD 675 and it survived the fire of 1666 largely through the efforts of Admiral Penn, the father of colonizer William Penn. During the second world war of recent history it wasn't so fortunate; only the walls and tower remained partially standing after the bombing of London. The present building was reconstructed using what remained of the original. But at the time of our visit it also had a Japanese-Korean restaurant, probably not of the original.

Upon arrival we were not allowed to enter on account of a service going on. It was hard to shake that pesky tourist mindset. There it was,

Sunday, and we expected the church to be open and available for us. It turned out to be a good time for a bite at one of the shops outside the entry to the Tower, only a block away. We returned to the church at the recommended time, but before we got too far inside the priest held us up. He had a fun time quizzing the kids with historical questions and giving us interesting information. He explained the Blackfriars and the Grayfriars, previously a burning question in all our minds. The two were separate religious orders of the middle ages, not early rival gangs. The Blackfriars wore black robes, the Grayfriars wore ... We all failed miserably on his historical questions. For example, which American president was married in All-Hallows Church? Of course, John Quincy Adams, the 6th president. Ok, then an easy one. What early American leader was baptized and schooled there? Simple, William Penn, son of Admiral Penn. At the least we gave the priest the smug pleasure of confirming his opinion of his nation's school system's preeminence over ours.

Once we did make it to the chamber down below we weren't overly impressed. True, there were some artifacts from Roman times, but the Roman road display was underwhelming. Mostly the space was a mausoleum for distinguished soldiers killed in the two world wars. In spite of all the Saxon crosses and model ships, it was a quick see.

After our time at the Globe and All-Hallows we only had what remained of the afternoon to tour the British Museum. Whatever were we thinking? Oh well. The Tube didn't have any obvious stops near to the Museum, so we wound up doing an extended walk through some interesting parts of London. We found ourselves among all world types of peoples: from Asia, the Middle East, Africa, India, and who knows where else. Striding briskly down the sidewalk we mingled with business people, street people, startling youth, school kids in uniforms, merchants hawking wares, gawking tourists, etc. I was amused by a van that was parked right up on the sidewalk. It was covered with Hebrew writing and was surrounded by a group of what could have only been Hasidic Jews (dark suits, hats, and long hair in locks) handing out flyers and talking with the people. Was it possibly a Jewish missionary event? We didn't pause to hear the golden question. It might have been entertaining, but we walked on.

A welcome aspect of most of the museums in England was the free admission. Donations were always welcomed and we did pitch in. In 1753 an act of Parliament established the British Museum as the world's first public museum. It was started with a purchase of the collection of Sir Hans Sloan, a Chelsea doctor. He had amassed over 80,000 curios—fossils, plants, coins, models, and prints. In 1757 George II presented the Royal Library to the museum and in 1823 George III gave the museum the right to a copy of every book ever printed. For more than two centuries the Museum has been collecting artifacts from all parts of the world.

So how were we going to fit in the viewing of over six million items? Time would certainly be a factor, but what was left of our endurance would be even more critical. We started by heading for the farthest corner of the building, the Asian exhibit. The room we entered, and several more above it, were filled with Chinese pottery and utensils, Japanese art, Indian (Asian) statues, and replicas of early Korean homes. Georgia had taken Chinese history in school and was intrigued with the representations of life in the Orient. The rest of us were inundated by teacups, coins, Buddha, Ganesh, pots, paintings, chopsticks, and on and on.

By the time we entered the Egyptian exhibit the crowd was picking up, evidently this was a popular stop. The room was loaded with mummies and sarcophagi; creating the possibility that currently England has more mummies on display than Egypt. The kids were especially intrigued with the shriveled body in the sand. It showed how the arid desert provided the initial conditions for mummification. But our problem became the overabundance of living bodies in the aisles.

We went to the exhibit of the early inhabitants of the English Isles and northwestern Europe. In many ways this exhibit was more interesting than the others. These mysterious, barbaric people were only mentioned in the historical writings of Rome and Egypt, the centers of learning and culture. But they are our ancestors and my how we have changed, in ways. Still, Tim's legs were giving out and the rest of us were just as beat. To save the group we decided to make for an exit and find a place to eat. Problem was, we couldn't find the exit. Room led to room after room before we could finally see the main hall again. Once outside we rested on the steps before pushing on.

It was a long hike to another Tube stop and after a short ride we got off to take a walk through St. James's Park. It was a lovely setting. Families were strolling and picnicking as we walked the bridge over the lake and from there toward Buckingham Palace. This wasn't going to be our chance to get a glimpse of royalty, we were not in a mood to wait and watch. We stopped across the street from the palace gates and took a few pictures from the distance. I'm sure it would have been a sight to watch some stuffy men in red and black suits perform the changing of the guard by marching precisely to and from a little box. At that moment we wanted to be the beef eaters.

On our walk back toward our B&B we chanced upon a Tandoori restaurant. Sitting down and eating such good food was just what we needed. After returning to our rooms we crashed into our beds for the final night in London. For me it was a bittersweet moment. Sure, I was ready to be out of the busy city, but from then on I would be driving. AAAAAH! I was not eagerly anticipating driving foreign roads in foreign cars abiding by foreign rules.

I have often commented since how glad I was to leave London. In looking back, however, I am sure I would actually enjoy visiting there again. Most of the negativity I felt was due to our own self-imposed busyness. We were new to the international-tourist way of bustling to a famous site, looking about quickly, making sounds of wonder and amusement, and then hurrying off to the next predetermined target. It was unavoidable; we had a lot to see in a limited time, and that pace pretty well continued throughout the rest of the trip. Needless to say, there is so much more to London than what we glimpsed. After all, it is a large, world city, a city that has been there for a long time. My opinion of London has mellowed somewhat by now and I would definitely include a less rushed stop there on my next England trip.

# DAY FOUR: *Roundabout Oxford*

I was a youngster when the James Bond phenomenon hit the States. Every kid had to have a spy attaché case and we dreamed of the cars with all the cool gadgets a spy would use. The 'cold war' was hot. Spy novels by Ian Fleming and John Le Carre were read by all. In Oxford I allowed myself a moment of spy fantasy.

◆　　　◆　　　◆

Everything had gone smoothly so far. All our gear had been safely hidden shortly after our arrival. Initial contact had been made and the key figures located. The scheduled departure time was not for a few more hours. In the meanwhile we attempted to fit in with the surrounding crowds as we tried desperately to solve the puzzle presented to us. It seems the royal family had a deep involvement in the matter. First an important offer had been refused. Then after certain information had been made public, a murder had 'happened'. Even our own government had wanted us to find out which side of the road we were on.

After seeing what was left of the body we began to see the picture. The church had not been a protection and it was a known fact that the alleged murderers had been closely associated with the monarchy. But what, or who, had prompted them? The more we looked about the more we sensed that so many other stories had their beginnings here. This was obviously a high level training facility we were viewing. The names of some of the more well-known individuals were freely obtained. These included David John Moore Cornwell of espionage repute, John Wesley with his army connection, and even Bill Clinton. Many were illustrious in their line, while others had turned out laughable. Even one of our own government had trained here. Could he be trusted? What if his cover were to be blown? Such questions.

We then separated for our final connections. One team went to the left, hopefully serving as a distraction for the other. I followed just a few steps behind the team that was going to pick up the items at the weapons of war shop. Still everything was going as planned. Just a bit more and we would be safely on our way, or so we hoped.

Then I saw it. Someone had spotted the two in front of me. I watched as he looked carefully at them and identification was made. He made a subtle signal to another that was with him. I knew there would not be much time for me to react. I still hoped we could make our contact without too much of a scene on the streets. But then the hooligan made his move. Stepping between my team and me he lengthened his stride. I mean he really changed his walk. He stepped out with an exaggerated, lanky, 'keep on truckin' type of gait. He swaggered his hips and shoulders. I was stunned, but then I watched, too. Sure enough, Americans walk funny.

◆    ◆    ◆

Georgia and I were the only ones at the table for the FEB that last morning in London. We were mindful of the energy we would be expending that day and besides, we had already paid for the meal, might as well eat it. The coffee and tea did make for a good start to the day. We checked out of the B&B and hauled our stuff the four blocks to the bus station. After locating the desired bus schedule posted on the wall, we purchased tickets for an express to Oxford and sat down for a short wait in the terminal. We had to carefully choose our seats because the open building allowed free entry to the pigeons. The bus soon pulled up, our bags were stowed, and we climbed aboard.

It was a relatively brief ride. I was determined to enjoy every bit of it because from Oxford on I would be behind the wheel. After leaving the motorway, the bus rolled down a small road into the town of Oxford. There it wound along smaller streets, amazing us that such a large bus could fit and maneuver through the narrow roads. Once it pulled into the station, we disembarked and asked directions to the address of the car rental agency. From this point we were out of London, seeing England, real world travelers. At the agency we learned a car wouldn't be available to us until the afternoon. However, the fellow at the desk allowed us to stash our bags there while we went to see the town. I was quite willing to postpone my encounter with driving until later.

We struck off on foot to see the town of Oxford. During the times of Saxon occupation, from 400–500 AD until the Norman conquest of the 11th century, the settlement was known as Ohsnafordia. There have been indications of scattered groups of inhabitants before then, but nothing too specific. John Rous, a historian during medieval times, claimed it had originally been settled by descendants of Noah, the Floater. Still others have said it was where a group of misplaced Trojans settled, no joke needed.

The settlement long served as a buffer between the Anglo-Saxon inhabitants of southern England and the invading Danes, the Vikings. Over time a large Danish population developed as many decided to quit invading and settled in. Talk about legal immigration issues. In 1002 AD a large fire occurred in the city and the Danish sector was given the blame for it and many were massacred. The still-practicing Vikings then sacked the town in 1009 as retribution, and one more time for good measure in 1013, under the leadership of Swein Forkbeard.

The town has known tension and violence for most of its existence. After the Viking/Dane issue it became the Reformists vs. Royalists during the Reformation and Civil War. The college in the town was staunchly Royalist and the townsfolk were predominantly Reformist. Just prior to the hostilities of this period was the occurrence of the most famous incident. On St. Scholastrica's day, February 10, 1354, an argument over 'indifferent' wine that was allegedly served at Swyndlestock Tavern spiraled out of control. Those damned students. The townsfolk came to the defense of the innkeeper and what followed were 3 days of fighting, beating, killing, and the ransacking of buildings. However, it was the townsfolk that were on the rampage. After things settled down, the city had to pay for repairs to the damaged college buildings and even into the Victorian era the Mayor of the city was required to swear allegiance to the University Chancellor each year in an extravagant ceremony. This was just further proof muggles and wizards cannot get along.

The University is what we readily associate with Oxford. The University is over 800 years old, having been described in writings of the late 1100's. There is no single university campus, but rather 36 independent colleges spread throughout the town. The colleges themselves are rather small, the largest having slightly more than 400 students and the smallest near 200. Their real estate holdings are large, due in large part to the practice of buying vast tracts of newly vacated properties during the years of plague outbreaks.

Here are a few tidbits about some of the colleges and grads of note.

Balliol College, 1263. Founded by the widow of John Balliol, contender of Robert the Bruce to the Scottish crown. The widow was a princess of Galloway with the catchy name of Dervorguilla, sadly not found in current baby name books.

Christ Church, 1525. Grads include early American founder William Penn and writer C. L. Dodgson (Lewis Carroll).

Braesenose College, 1509. So named because of the Brazen Nose doorknocker on its entry door. It resembles the snout of an animal and I can think of no better way to choose a name for an institution of higher learning.

Exeter College, 1314. Past students include actor Richard Burton and J. R. R. Tolkein.

Herteford College, 1282. It was dissolved and recreated on a number of occasions. 17<sup>th</sup> century poet John Donne and Jonathan Swift (*Gulliver's Travels*) attended.

Jesus College, 1571. Founded by none other than ... no wait, it was by some other guys, and not even apostles at that. A grad of note was T. E. Lawrence (of Arabia).

Kellogg College, 1994. This one was founded by the namesake.

Lincoln College, 1427. John Wesley, founder of Methodism and the Salvation Army, got his inspiration here. Others were John Le Carre (spy novels) and Dr. Seuss (why spy I books).

Magdelen College, 1458. Playwright Oscar Wilde, novelist C. S. Lewis, and actor Dudley Moore were grads.

Somerville College, 1879. Founded by Mary Somerville to give women an opportunity for higher education at Oxford. Grads of this school include Indian Prime Minister Indira Gandhi and Prime Minister of England Margaret Thatcher.

St. John's College, 1555. Attended by the just stepped down British Prime Minister Tony Blair.

University College, 1249. Yet another politician, Bill Clinton.

The Queen's College, 1341. Rowan Atkinson. Mr. Bean goes to college.

We were planning on visiting only one of the colleges, Christ Church. It required a walk across town from where the bus had dropped us. After walking three blocks into the town proper, we all had a chance to satisfy our addictions. Georgia and I had frappucinos at a cyber café. Upstairs from us Kara and Chris had the first chance to send emails back home. Just next-door was a Games Workshop, where Tim looked over Warhammer pieces, small warrior figures that were to be painted and used for playing battle games.

Thus satisfied, we went to Christ Church College, with its cathedral being our primary interest and occupying most of our time there. Within the cathedral were a number of smaller chapels dedicated to various historic and religious figures. One such shrine supposedly contained the relics of St. Frideswide under a canopy. She is the patron saint of Oxford. According to legend she fled the marriage advances of a local ruler and found refuge in the area. Once he found her and was just about to grasp her, he was struck blind. It was after his repentance of his desires for her that she granted his sight back. She wasn't that into blind dating.

Another wing of the Christ Church cathedral contained a stained glass window, from the early 1300's, depicting the assassination of Thomas Beckett, the Archbishop of Canterbury appointed by King Henry II. He accumulated the King's disfavor by publicly announcing and opposing many of the ruler's actions. Though they had started as friends, he so vexed the King that it is said in a fit of frustration Henry bellowed out loud something to the effect, "Who will rid me of this menace?" A number of loyal, and favor-seeking, nobles led by a Sir Guido and Lord Vinny, decided to make it so. Afterward Henry was struck by much remorse and performed many acts of penance. He had many images of Beckett destroyed, but had the glass in Christ Church created.

After leaving the cathedral we walked through the college dining hall. It was a large, spacious room with three long rows of oak tables and chairs. Just try to picture the dining scenes from the *Harry Potter* movies. Actually, that was where the scenes from the first movie were filmed.

From the Christ Church campus we strolled alleys and side streets to the Radcliffe Camera. Camera is a medieval word meaning 'room'. The building is a large, 16-sided, half-dome shaped reading room that serves the underground Bodleian Library, one of the world's greatest and largest, with 117 miles of shelving. It was built in the mid-1700's and the architecture was inspired by the Tower of Winds in Hellenic Athens. A sign posted outside informed us the building was only for student use, no tourists. We were content with a couple of family pictures of us with it as a background.

After a quick bite we split up. Georgia and Kara went to the post to mail some cards. I followed the boys back to the Games Workshop. This was where I was walking a few yards behind the two when I saw a young fellow just ahead of me nudge his girlfriend and point to the backs of Chris and Tim. I tensed up, expecting some sort of mischief from this fellow and watched as he mimicked their way of walking. I relaxed and chuckled. I don't know if our wide-open country fosters a different walk from that of folks in a country bound on an island, but it is distinctly different.

The moment I had been dreading was fast approaching. We met up again and headed back toward the auto rental office. One last diversion presented itself just before we got back to the office. An Abbey Road street sign had to be used for a photo op. It was not the one of Beatle fame, but it would do.

Our car awaited us. It was a new Peugeot, 5 person, 4 doors, with standard transmission. I was troubled since shifting would be done with the left hand, but at least the foot pedals were the same as I was used to. As we filled out the paperwork, the agent tried to be reassuring.

"Really, we don't have many wrecks with tourists."

I was glad he was confident because I was not. What if we were the exception? We fit everything snugly into the boot, what we knew as the trunk, and then went for a test drive down a side street in the neighborhood. It didn't really ease my fears any. Driving from the right side of the car and trying to stay on the left side of the road was so strange. We came to the main road and shut our eyes. Simple, turn right and move over to the left lane. All of us with a driver's license were tense, while Tim in his naiveté wasn't worried at all. A traveling arrangement evolved that worked for us. I would drive and concentrate on staying to the left. The person in the passenger seat was to keep track of directions, distances, road numbers, signs, turn-offs, etc. Georgia sat in the middle in the back seat. She was to grab the knee of each person beside her and squeeze at appropriately tense moments. For the first few days that would have been the entire time on the road, at least for me. I was doing my own squeezing that day.

Our first goal on the map was the town of Swindon where we would then get on the M4, a main highway like the I-5 at home. While still on the smaller road we frequently encountered the as yet unfamiliar and dreaded roundabout. That would occur at any major, or minor, intersection. There was no stoplight or stop sign other than at the entry to the circle. I had to watch right, not left, get into the outer lane of the circle, and be ready to zip off as we circled to the appropriate exit. We got pretty good at navigating through those traffic challenges, having to repeat the circle on only one or two occasions. After that, being on the M4 was like being on any freeway here, just driving and staying to the left, unless we were passing, and that involved pulling to the right.

The agent at the car rental in Oxford had recommended we take a break at a rest stop just beyond Swindon. That would give rush hour traffic around Bristol a chance to settle down. The stop was nice enough. There were shops, fast food establishments, and restrooms—er, toilets. We feasted on hamburgers, chicken sandwiches, and fries. This was one of the few times we found and welcomed some familiar fast foods.

Georgia struck up a conversation with two of the maintenance workers in the building. I listened in just to hear their accents. When she told them we planned to travel through Wales on up to Conway they both agreed that would be quite a trip. One of them was from Scotland, a foreigner himself. The other had never ventured that far from his home. Can you imagine not ever having traveled 200 miles from your home? How we think nothing of a trip across the wide-open spaces of the USA.

The rental agent had also warned us about the bridge we would cross over the Severn River just past Bristol. He described it in a frightening manner; high, narrow, no side rails. I was disappointed. I-5 into Portland, Oregon, is much worse; he would perish of the fright. On the Severn Bridge my main anxiety was locating the proper exit. Our

B&B was located in Sedbury, on the English side of the border with Wales. To get there we would have to pass through Chepstow, which straddled the border. From there the house was just outside of town in a country setting at the end of a turn off on a small road decorated with the occasional cow-pie in the center. There we were actually in someone's home. An unheated outdoor pool was available and we made use of it. Again, we had two bedrooms and there were two bathrooms down the hall.

That evening we enjoyed being able to chat with the hostess for a few moments. At one point we were discussing our travel plans for the next day. Originally we had planned to drive into Bath and join the other hundreds of tourists for the day. She suggested instead of seeing "touristy" Bath, that we should see the sights in the Chepstow area. An impressive castle was in town and Tintern Abbey was only a few minutes away. We had wanted to somehow see the abbey, so we altered our plans accordingly and hit the hay. Kara was pleased by the occasional sound of a horse clopping by on the road outside.

# DAY FIVE: *It's Digestible*

In the early 1100's Geoffrey of Monmouth presented a book titled *History of the kings of Britain*. It was a bestseller at the time and was considered to be an accurate history for many years. Although the veracity of its contents has not held up to subsequent research, it is still considered one of the most influential books to have come out of Britain. Having made submissions to publishers, I must wonder what Geoffrey may have had to go through to be published.

◆　　◆　　◆

"Look, Geoffrey, everyone wants to write a history-of-Britain type book right now. The market is flooded. Our monks are busy 24/7 copying the one we have going at the moment. If you really want to get in, then this work needs to be something different."

"What if I call it a history of the kings of Britain?"

"That is not anything new. All the histories cover the kings. Who else is there to talk about?"

"Ok. What if I have a different opening? Like, say I reveal the first king as a Trojan? I could make the first settlers on the island to be Trojan wanderers."

"Are you making this up? Remember, this is billed as a history."

"No, really. I read this in a book the archbishop gave me. And what if we loosely call it a history; say it is based on some facts?"

"Well, maybe. What else have you got on it?"

"I can tie in some of the local Welsh legends. Nobody really knows or cares if they are true or not. Besides, the locals would love the connection."

"True. They are still sensitive about the Normans taking over. It might ease their pain. But then it would only have local appeal. It needs more."

"What I was thinking was I could use one of the favorite characters from the legends. I'll even borrow bits from some other legends, like the Scottish, or Irish, or even the French. Then I would carefully rearrange some of the 'facts' so that he is a part of each of the groups on the island."

"Yeah, yeah. Tell me more."

"If you remember from my first book about Merlin, the Welsh really adored this Arthur character I put in it. So I will make him bigger in this book. We'll call him the King, not of Wales only, or of Scotland, or even of just the Britons, but of England. I'll place him far enough back in time and in an unidentifiable place called Camelot. I'll make him the model of justice and truth, what a king should aspire to rule as. Why, I'll even throw in some romance and adventure to liven it up."

"Now you're talking. But if this is a 'true history', then why is there no Camelot or court of King Arthur around any more?"

"Okay. I have a killer of a handkerchief ending. Someone close to him betrays Arthur and as a result his kingdom is swept away, not a stone or record remains. That way we don't have to prove his existence, he becomes legend."

"Geoff, I think you might have a story for us. Send me a draft as soon as you have one and I'll put our readers to work."

"Thank you, Robert. By the way, do you think you could mention my name in court? Or at least arrange some sort of advance for me?"

"Ha! Writers. I'll see what I can do. But remember I get a fair percentage."

◆        ◆        ◆

It was our first morning out of London, a different cook, a different kitchen, a different dining room, but still the same eggs, bacon, tomatoes, mushrooms, and fried toast. It was a good thing we would be doing a lot of walking.

It was just the second day of driving, but we were already getting a feel for it. The first excursion of the morning would be north of the town of Chepstow to Tintern Abbey. Monmouth, the birthplace of Geoffrey, was only a little farther up the same road past the abbey, but we were not planning on going that far. We had not heard of that 12th century historical fiction writer yet. But we were eager to see Tintern. Fortunately it was a quiet drive on the road and in only five minutes we were exiting the trees and coasting down into the wide valley formed by the Wye River. A decrepit, stone structure loomed just ahead of us. There were only a couple of cars in the parking lot. As we approached the small building at the entrance, we had our first exposure to the Welsh language. The sign over the door greeted visitors first in Welsh and then in English.

Tintern Abbey was erected by monks of the Cistercian order in the 12th century. The Cistercians were the essence of austerity. Monasteries were typically located far from the towns of the time in order to limit contact with the outside world. The monks there were known as 'white monks', different from the Blackfriars of the London area. This was on account of the plain, un-dyed wool garments they wore. They had brought sheep into the area for that purpose and, as they were slowly contaminated by the world, for trade. The Cistercians played a large role in establishing the wool industry in Wales. In spite of their initial desire to be far from the pagan world, it was their wool trade that encouraged the growth of communities nearby. The abbey was not only sought out for its wool, but was also a shelter for the sick and those traveling through the area. As its utility and prestige increased, additions were made to the original structure through the 15th century.

In 1348, an episode of Black Death in England curtailed the growth of the abbey. It was impossible to entice new recruits to serve God when so many were already on their way to see him. The Plague changed the economy of the area so that most of the locations that were formerly farmed and sheeped by lay brethren were rented to tenants.

As severe as the Plague was, it was another epidemic that was responsible for the dissolution of the monastery way of life. Just like the Plague, the Reformation had swept the continent. During the reign of King Henry VIII, the Dissolution of Monasteries ended a way of life for many. The Act of Supremacy of 1534 placed the King of England second only to God in matters of governing, both secular and theological. Henry VIII, Cardinal Wolsey, and Secretary Thomas Cromwell, progenitor to Oliver Cromwell, accomplished the dissolution and eventual destruction of over 800 buildings, almost all the Catholic cathedrals and monasteries on the island. Some historians have suggested it wasn't so much Henry that was determined to carry out such sweeping actions, but rather his staunchly protestant ministers. Now why does that sound too familiar? On September 3, 1536, Tintern Abbey was surrendered to the King's visitors. It was not destroyed, but uninhabited. The roof was removed for the use of its lead, the windows were broken out for the glass, and occasionally some of the stones were used for local habitations. Ultimately it was time that wore down the building. What remains today is a large skeleton of what was once a very impressive establishment. Actually, it is still impressive.

Our tour began in what were once the quarters of the monks and brethren that supported the abbey. All that was left for viewing were the remnants of walls and the smooth stone floors where monks slept, ate, learned, gardened, tended the sick, and latrined. It was engaging to wander among the ruins, guidebook in hand, and imagine what life could have been like then. Tim, Georgia, and I had read most of the

*Redwall Abbey* books of the time and could easily picture the inhabitants busying about.

The roof of the church was missing and the windows were all gone, but the walls still stood. The carpet of grass on the inside was a patchwork of shadows and sunshine formed by the missing parts. I would say I was as awe struck there as at St. Paul's in London. Artists were scattered at various viewpoints around the building capturing the aspects of the chapel on canvas. But lacking such time luxury ourselves, we inhaled a bit of the moment and hurried on. Tintern Abbey was definitely one of the highlights of the trip. When asked later what were his favorite sights, Tim confirmed that the Abbey was his favorite.

Once back in Chepstow we made a tour of the castle around which the town was built. Unlike the Tower of London, crowds here were not a problem. We were given a freer reign of the site. The castle was erected, and added to, as a long narrow group of structures sitting atop a cliff along the River Wye. It provided a fun, mostly leisurely ramble through old rooms, across grassy baileys, along crumbling parapets, and even up decrepit, slippery, spiral stairways. It was near the end of our castle tour that we attempted the stairs of the massive Marten's Tower. It was interesting to learn the tower was not named for its prominent financer and occupant, Earl Roger Bigod, but rather for Henry Marten, a prisoner kept there for signing the death warrant of King Charles I. That was a reminder to carefully read all contracts and circulating petitions before signing them.

The castle had been originally started, around 1046, near an ancient iron age fort and was meant to serve as a base for the newly arrived, conquering Normans to deal with the Welsh. In time the English name for the place, Cheap-Stow—market town, came to replace the original Welsh name, Ystraigyl—bend of the river. Neither was very unique, but the Welsh sure looked like a tongue twister. There had been four stages of construction. Marten's Tower was one of the last structures built, and standing several stories tall it offered a commanding view of the surrounding area and of the rest of the castle. In case of internal problems it could be self-sufficient and self-defended. The spiral stairway was our challenge. We carefully made the climb, pausing at each succeeding level to peer into the empty space and imagine the difference it would make to have the wooden floors in place to provide the living quarters for the early inhabitants. The problems we encountered with the stairway were the lack of handrails, the narrow steps, the state of disrepair, and the occasional student of a tour group zipping past.

After the castle we went into the town and wandered for a bit. There was not too much to see there, or maybe the shops were closed for the moment. It was mid-afternoon when we returned to the B&B. The kids went for the pool again and Georgia and I took a hike into Sedbury to find a market. We bought yogurt, fruit, bread, and cheese for an evening meal. We had originally planned on purchasing more of our meals this way in the hopes of cutting some costs. Markets weren't that easy to locate and restaurants were just so much more convenient. One item we saw on the shelf in this market was a package of digestibles, a cookie/cracker that Georgia had run into when she was in London a few years earlier. We included one in our purchase and took everything back to the B&B. When the kids saw the term 'digestibles' on the package they wanted nothing to do with them. They affectionately called them 'bis-squirts'.

As Rick Steves had recommended, we were traveling light, and as a result it was time to get a load of laundry done. Georgia and I drove back in to Chepstow to find a laundromat. Even though the town was rather small it took us some time to locate one and by that time it was just closing. We would be leaving early the next morning, so we were out of luck. We decided to plan a stop in Aberystwyth, a town on the way to our next destination, Porthmadog. Looking for Porthmadog on the map and seeing how small it appeared we were concerned about the availability of a laundromat there.

The prospects of the next day had us somewhat daunted. The road trip itself promised to be lengthy and now a few hours laundry stop would be needed. Ahhh, but we were really going to be in Wales, not merely at the border.

# DAY SIX: Country Road

The north Wales legend of 13<sup>th</sup> century Prince Llewelyn and his dog gives a sense of the passion of the Welsh and the tragedy they have endured through centuries of English dominance. That and it really gets PETA riled up.

Llewelyn was an avid hunter and loved nothing better than taking his dogs into the Snowdonia Mountains to hunt. His favorite dog was Gelert, a fearless hunter, loyal friend, and companion. On one fateful hunt the wife of Llewelyn accompanied him and his Irish wolfhounds, leaving their son in the care of a servant and their nurse. True to the fairy tale formula, the nurse and servant decide to go for a walk, or a cavort more likely, in the forest and leave the baby alone and unprotected.

Before too long, Llewelyn notices Gelert is missing from the pack. He knows the only place the dog would go is home and suspecting mischief, he calls off the hunt and races home. As they approach home they are greeted by a bloodstained Gelert, his tail wagging happily. They rush into the house to find the cradle overturned and bloody bedclothes scattered about, but no sign of the baby. Overcome by rage and grief Llewelyn drives his sword through his dog. As Gelert dies he whimpers and his sounds bring forth the sound of a baby crying from behind the cradle. Throwing aside the cradle they find their baby unharmed, but the bloody body of a huge wolf lies next to him. Gelert had killed the wolf.

Filled with a deep sorrow, Llewelyn buries the body of his faithful Gelert in a nearby meadow. The village that grew there is Beddgelert, 'burial place of Gelert'.

◆     ◆     ◆

Since our B&B was on the English side of the border and our hosts were English, breakfast was still full English. The novelty was long gone already and even the humor was wearing thin. There would be no Arby's along the way, so we ate what we could. Even I was less inclined to finish off everyone else's breakfast, already paid for or not.

We were on the road again, but there were no major roadways on this portion of the trip. The two-lane roads took us through lovely country and through quaint, small towns. Their names were fun to consider the lingual contortions of pronouncing: Aberhonddu, Llan-fair-ym-Muallt, Rhaeadr, Llangurig. These had Puyallup and Sno-qualmie beat by a long shot.

After just a couple of hours of narrow roads and round-abouts, we finally found our way into Aberystwyth shortly after noon. The town of Aberystwyth was founded as a garrison town to support the Norman conquest of the locals. Remains of an Iron Age fort on a nearby hill suggest the area has had a significant importance for many centuries. It is presently a lively city with a university population during the school year and an influx of tourists in the summer. Maybe that explains why many of the local businesses posted alcohol sales and the repair of bro-ken shop windows as two of the services they offered. One website was eager to claim there were *only* fifty pubs left in the city.

After a drive through downtown we located a parking area in front of a supermarket-like establishment. After putting a pound or two into the meter we took the bags of laundry for a six block hike back down-town to where we thought we had spotted a laundromat on our way in. Sure enough, there was a little one near the end of the main street through town. Once the washers were loaded we decided to backtrack to an Italian restaurant nearby. We still weren't quite sure of the English food serving schedule and hoped it would be open. We were the only patrons at the moment, but food was still being served.

Admittedly, it was a trifle difficult to sit and relax at a meal while our only clothes were a few minutes away and all by themselves. Georgia felt it most acutely and rushed her meal. I was more concerned about our time limit for parking running out. Georgia and the kids went for the clothes and I went the other direction to feed the meter another pound. It was an experience walking through town all by myself. I couldn't help but wonder if people were aware I was a foreigner, if there was some subtle clue that I was strange. You may ask why I don't entertain the same question here at home, where the clues are not subtle at all. Well, regardless of my strangeness, we didn't want to end up missing our clothes and our car in Aberystwyth. Once both missions were accomplished we loaded back into the car and continued on our way.

I must say that, over all, driving in England was not as extremely stressful as I had imagined. With that said, two portions did push me to my limits. We can talk about Edinburgh later, but it was the small roads in Wales that gave me a new appreciation for those small cars of which we had previously made fun. The roads were not overly wide and most of the time there was virtually no shoulder to speak of. There were stretches of road where a stone wall marked the side of the road. It wouldn't be a respectable few feet to the side, but right at the side. And most often at such a stretch a truck, lorry, would be coming at us from the other direction. Those lorries were just as large as the ones here. So each encounter was a brief moment of panic. The kids were entertained by my involuntary Tourette-like outbursts. Before long I was so looking forward to the end of the day's drive. It was good everyone else had a chance to see more of the rustic countryside than I did.

Passing through the small towns was a whole other dilemma. Within the town there would be no curbside parking in front of the businesses for patrons to leave their cars. The town center was usually only a few buildings long, but a car was always just stopped in the road in front of a shop, effectively reducing the road to one lane only. Oncoming traffic would have to figure whose turn it was to proceed.

Fortunately, the drivers we met in that way were all courteous and patient.

With only a couple of miles to our stop for the day, Porthmadog, I thought we had it made. At the start of the final half-mile stretch into town we had to pause at a toll collection station. It was the least official looking toll booth I had ever seen. Two guys were standing on either side of the road, buckets at their feet for the money collected. Folding chairs were there for resting during the slow moments. The posted fare was 5 pence, less than a dime at the time. We did our best to maintain a serious look because we thought it had to be some kind of a joke.

No, the joke was on us and it was the next 1/8-mile of road. The lane on our side was butted right up against a wall of rock; rough-hewn it loomed over us. The lane on the other side barely avoided falling down into the marsh several feet below. The traffic was steady, and busy, in both directions and there was no space to pull over and consider our fates. I had to drive right on. Surely that would be the place where at least one side mirror would be sacrificed. I was seriously considering which one it should be and getting it over with.

Miraculously, we escaped with all our protuberances intact and no wounds along the doors. Our B&B was just outside of the town center. However, it was well hidden in the trees a short drive off the road and the driveway was inconspicuous. We circled back and turned in. It would be like being in a cottage in the woods for the next two nights. Our host showed us up the wooden stairway to our rooms.

After a long day in the car it was refreshing to stretch our legs on the trail through the garden on the hillside next to the house. That warmed us up for the walk back into town. Did I say we did a lot of walking on the trip? At least our health had that going for it. After wandering up and down the main street, maybe four blocks, we ducked into a busy restaurant that had a local feel to it. Inside we noted the staff and most of the customers were speaking in an unrecognizable language, their Welsh. They would slip back and forth from Welsh to English as needed. We ordered lamb, or chicken, or beef with potatoes and dined with the locals.

Later, back at the B&B, the owner gave us recommendations for the next day's sites. All the guidebooks noted there were castles aplenty in the area. We mentioned Harlech and asked what he would advise.

"Oh, so you want to see an 'English' castle?" The disdainful way he said 'English' informed us with no reservation what his opinion of the denizens to the east was. It was obvious this sentiment was prevalent throughout this northwestern corner of Wales. The Welsh had been picked on enough. Descended from what we call today the Celtic people of Europe, they didn't invade England as a group, but rather wandered over bits at a time and mingled in with or displaced the Neolithic inhabitants. The Romans campaigned across the island and set up their centers of rule. They especially disliked the Druids, the Celtic priests, and all but eliminated them. When the Saxons came over they proved less invasive and less inclusive. The Normans were just plain conquerors, literally medieval butt-heads.

"King Edward was a very, very bad man," he said with a grimace. The late 13th century king (of *Braveheart* fame) had harshly put down a rebellion by the Welsh. To solidify his hold on the land he had a number of castles constructed such that the remaining rebels were contained high in the Snowdonia Mountains.

"Criccieth is a fine Welsh castle." We put it first on our list. How could we do otherwise? A peaceful sleep in the Welsh forest was welcome. A deep slumber from the times of dark, druidic mysteries enveloped us like a mist as chanting nature outside our windows closed our eyes. Not really, we were just tired.

# DAY SEVEN: Harlech and Hooligans

The 12th century saw another notable Welsh author, Gerald of Wales. Since his father was a Norman knight and his mother was the daughter of a Norman lord and Welsh princess, he had both Welsh and Norman blood. His mixed ancestry made him an asset to the English rulers and he served often as an advisor to the King on Welsh affairs. A well-educated man, he was a lecturer on Civil and Canon (church) Law at the University of Paris. He also traveled extensively and wrote about his forays through the Welsh countryside. Seventeen of his books have survived the centuries and because of their accounts we quite possibly know more about him than any other person of that time.

It was the passion Gerald felt for the Welsh church that fueled his life and thwarted his desires. The Welsh had brought Christianity to the Saxons of England. Gerald felt the Welsh church had withered under Norman rule. It was his opinion that the church at St. David's, located on the coast west of Cardigan and the center of the church in Wales, should be independent of the church at Canterbury and that it should have its own Archbishop who reported directly to Rome.

Somewhere along the way Gerald had made a staunch enemy of the Archbishop of Canterbury. He had accused the Archbishop of stockpiling arms and selling them for inflated prices to Crusaders, a supplier of weapons of medieval destruction. It was this enemy at Canterbury that sabotaged his every effort to become the Archbishop of St. David's.

In his literary efforts Gerald displayed his political acumen by appealing to multiple sides in a conflict. In one of his books he had devoted a chapter to informing the Norman overlords how to effectively defeat the Welsh separatists. In a following chapter he turned around and gave his recommendations on how the Welsh could thwart such attempts.

When Gerald had a second chance at the Archbishopric he was assured the title by King John, whom he had tutored as a child. So he made the arduous trek to Rome to be ordained by the Pope. But Canterbury had been ahead of him with a smear campaign and the liberal use of funds. He was denied the post again and made the sad journey home. At this point it was obvious he would never get the appointment. And those trips to Rome had worn him out physically. He retired to a monastery and lived a long life of 77 years.

I have heard a stand-up comic, Gaffigan?, asking if we wondered when the Pope was a child did he dream of becoming the Pope. We all laugh because that sounds absurd. An account of Gerald's childhood relates how while his brothers would be building sandcastles at the beach, he would be building sand churches. He had to have been loads of fun to play games with. And he probably did dream of being the Pope.

◆     ◆     ◆

It was sad to see the Welsh breakfast had been conquered by the English, too. The eggs and bacon smouldered with contempt. Still, I can't imagine how Welsh lamb could have been prepared for a breakfast, not unless one considers Scotland and the culinary things they did to sheep.

Pulling out of the driveway to the B&B we turned toward the west, where Criccieth was located, or where we thought it was. A short while later we drove onto the beach on Cardigan Bay, obviously lost. The beach entrance fee collector, complete with folding chair and bucket for money, told us of a shortcut back to the proper road. We wound up, down, and around on a very narrow, one-lane road. I was so relieved we met no traffic; even a lone sheep would have blocked our progress. We had to have a picture of that road, and that is the one I like to show friends when I talk about driving the roads in Wales.

Criccieth is a quaint village of stone cottages. The castle sits on the top of a rise on the beach. The castle, like many of its time, is pretty broken down. Here a lot of the destruction was not due to the ravages of time, or a foreign army, but the last Welsh occupants, a rowdy group on tour. The castle, originally built by the Welsh, was held alternately by the Welsh and the English. The English held it more because they could provision it from the sea for indefinite periods. During the last Welsh uprising, a sympathic French fleet happened to be sitting offshore, thus preventing the arrival of English provisions. Once it was in their hands, the Welsh forces, frustrated with the English using their fortified crib, dismantled and razed the structure. It was a definite instance of NIMBY.

As it was early, we virtually had the castle to ourselves. Within the ticket office was a fine exhibit of early life and affairs. Up to that time it was difficult to separate the societies of the Welsh and the English in my mind. I wouldn't say that to anyone of Welsh descent now. A large segment of the exhibit was a fun, animated presentation chronicling the travels of Gerald of Wales around the principality. For this presentation he was only billed as a local monk, but did get a bit part in the never-ending Crusades. We missed out on learning more fully of his true significance in Welsh history.

The Welsh, always used by the British military, see themselves as essential to other world events besides the Crusades and the squashing of Scotland. One source noted that the name for our continent, America, comes from a Welsh name, Amerik. Richard Amerik had financed the adventure of John Cabot, who sailed along the North American coast shortly before Vespucci sailed the South American coast. The name of Amerik on the maps Cabot fashioned from his trip would have given rise to it being called Amerik's land. It actually does make sense.

Our walk of the castle grounds was shorter than the film we had just watched in the ticket office. A splendid view was offered of the bay and the cottages across from the castle were too picturesque to not take a photo or two. In the distance we could discern the outline of the next castle we wanted to see, Harlech.

From Criccieth we made our way to the English castle. Since we had to pass over the toll road again, I closed my eyes and tolerated the narrow crossing and we made it again in one piece, thank you St. Christopher. For the duration of the ten-mile jaunt along the coast we could see the castle of Harlech, perched high atop a bluff overlooking the bay. We drove straight to the base of the bluff, where a lengthy stairway angled up to the castle. We parked in the small, almost empty lot, paid our fee in a small office, and made the climb up the 108 wide, shallow steps to the castle. After we had toured through the castle to the other side we saw the main entrance, complete with a larger information center and flight of only 10 steps. Sadly, Georgia had trekked back down the longer flight to the car and up again when we had gotten separated at one point during our tour of the grounds.

Compared to Criccieth, this castle was in much better repair. Wooden structures had disappeared, but the layout was easy enough to imagine. The gatehouse was in good shape and offered displays to get a glimpse of the daily operations. The stroll along the top of the walls was breezy, refreshing. While I was gazing over the view from the walls a man walked over and started a conversation with me. He said he was associated with the Welsh Heritage Association and was pleased to see an American family touring one of the nation's sites. He and his wife were also visiting, from south Wales and were interested to see what the 'north Welsh' had to offer. He made some point of the differences between the inhabitants of the north and the south, notably the language dialects. I forget what they were and I listened hard but couldn't hear any southern drawl on the guy.

After Harlech we made our final trip over the infamous toll road back into Porthmadog. Our next planned stop was the slate mines in

the mountains above the town. The slate was used as a building mate-
rial and Porthmadog had been settled to access, service, and provide
shipping for the mines. We booked on a steam train that was offered,
because of the novelty and to avoid passing over the toll road again.
We were able to catch the one that was just leaving and sat bunched in
a cabin with a traveler from Yorkshire, and his dog. It was a slow chug
up the mostly wooded mountain to the stop at Blaenau Ffestiniog. The
Welsh towns would not readily lend themselves to the cheers we hear
at our football games. How would a B-F cheer go?

We chugged into town and followed the crowd off the train and up
the stairs into the town. In the parking lot we watched as groups
boarded buses and rolled away. Once we were left on our own we figured the buses must have been the way to get to the mines. We had
visualized the train taking us more directly to the mines and were
reluctant to arrange another ride. Also, by the time we would have
toured the mine we would be cutting it close for what we imagined the
last train back was, according to the schedule we had consulted. We
decided to kick around town a bit and take the next train down.
Besides, we were hungry. Fortunately, a suitable looking deli was across
the street. After we seated ourselves and settled in we were told they
had just stopped serving lunch and were closing for the afternoon
break. ARGHHH! We wandered over to the old hotel and asked if
they were serving anything. The man at the door said only sandwiches
and drinks were available. One of us had a Welsh rarebit sandwich
(bread and cheese) and I forget what the rest of us had. Undoubtedly,
whatever we ordered turned out to be a variation of the same, bread
and cheese.

We admitted we were done for the day and took the next train
down. Back in town we made a brief trek to the local ATM, passing a
crowd of kids beating cans around with sticks. We all felt a little vul-
nerable, surrounded by Welsh hooligans, in Porthmadog. We made it
back to the B&B without any incident. Our time in Wales was draw-
ing to a close and aside from the hooligans; I had enjoyed the overall

atmosphere. It seemed more on the wild side of nature. As wild, that is, as a land occupied and worked for thousands of years can be. The Welsh, as a people, seemed more introverted, a quieter people. I admit I often felt more of a stranger, a foreigner there and could easily say it wasn't an entirely friendly or welcoming feeling.

It rained as we slept that night. We had been in Britain for seven days before experiencing the typical, island rains. That was pretty good, but we did hope our luck was not running out.

# DAY EIGHT: We Sack York

The discovery and exploration of the Americas made many significant new world finds available to those of the old world. The Swiss got their chocolate. Sir Walter Raleigh could fill his pipe with tobacco. The potato gave Germans their *kartoffelkopf* (potato head) and the Irish their potato famine. More important, the French invented freedom fries and the English chips for their fish.

The potato was a food crop originating in the Andes Mountains of South America. The native inhabitants of the high, cold, and arid mountains could not grow the crops of the lower elevations, beans and maize. However, the bitter little tubers that could be found as high as 15,000 feet could meet their nutritional needs. Over time they developed larger, tastier hybrids and the potato eventually became an important commodity for the tribes of South America. They had gods dedicated to the spud and included images of potatoes in their artwork. In some depictions the potatoes were given human features. The glasses, moustache, and bowler hat were later additions.

The Spanish conquistadors, during their looting raids, came across potatoes and even shipped some of the curiosities back to Spain. At the same time other explorers were returning with the potato to many countries of Europe. The initial response was very subdued. At first people were afraid of the plant because of its relation to the poisonous nightshade family. It was feared to cause leprosy, syphilis, and was thought to be a dangerous aphrodisiac. So naturally it was considered suitable for only the lower classes.

It was the practical Germans that realized the nutritional value of the plant. For growing it required less land and labor, and it contained several vital nutrients. The people came to depend on it for a food.

That was partly because King Fredrick William ordered peasants to plant and eat potatoes or have their noses sliced off. During the truly Teutonic "Potato War" two warring states, unable to achieve a military victory, sent their soldiers out to locate the enemy's potato crops and eat or destroy them.

During the Seven Years War, where Prussia and France were in conflict, a French physician, Parmentier, was a POW and while in prison he was served potato for all his meals. He was converted to spudism and on his return to Franc he tried to convince his countrymen of the value of the potato. No Frenchman wanted anything to do with that silly American root. So he planted a large field and posted a serious guard over it during the day. People took notice of the guard and would sneak into the field in the evening and liberate the obviously precious plants. Genius!

The potato enabled notable growth in city populations and fed the Industrial Revolution. It became very important in Ireland, where not as much land was readily available for cultivation of crops. Families would plant heaps of earth, known as 'lazy rows', and leave them alone until time for harvest. In other parts of Britain farmers got more serious about the crop. In the early 1700's, Jethro 'Thick as a Potato' Tull, an accomplished agriculturalist of the time, developed a plow solely for cultivating straight rows of potato plants.

All of this potato history brings us finally back to the gastronomic delight of English fish and chips. The web sites I searched gave me the impression the Brits are quite fond of their fish and chips. A respectable chip shop menu lists at least three or four different fish and chip combinations. Fish and chip eateries outnumber McDonalds in England by ten to one. They are serious.

So the question for us was, were we going to try an authentic fish and chips meal?

◆     ◆     ◆

Full Welsh/English Breakfast, may I never see fried eggs and ham again. On the road again and the morning segment of the drive was a joy. For one thing, we did not have to pass over the toll road that I detested so much, and also in a few miles we were on a main motorway again. There would be no more narrow, rock wall-lined roads. With a plethora of castles in the region, we decided to skip Caernarfon and Beaumaris and head for Conwy castle for our fill for the day. After a brief drive on the A55 motorway we took the Conwy exit and headed straight for the towering stone wall we could see from the highway. We found a parking space right at the wall and were quite pleased with ourselves for finding one so close. What we had so skillfully located was the town wall. The castle itself was about a mile away from where we entered the wall. Since the walk along the top of the wall led directly to the castle we just hiked on.

Just as Harlech castle was in better repair than Criccieth castle, Conwy castle was even better yet than Harlech. Much of the interior wall work was standing enough to allow us to imagine the apartments, halls, kitchens, stores, and chapel. Our camera was put to much use taking pictures from towers and walls, looking across wards, into dungeons, and through windows and other openings. The gift shop at the end was more of the same as the others. Frankly, after touring three castles in two days straight we were done with scrambling around old symbols of power and rule, for a while. So after leaving the castle we went to a shop across the street. They specialized in medieval costumes and weapons. Ok, we were not quite done with such symbols yet. We successfully resisted purchasing any swords and even passed on a costume photo opportunity.

Before climbing back into the car we needed to put something into our stomachs. A few doors down was a little outdoor café that was actually serving food, notably fish and chips. But we weren't yet ready for that particular dish. Georgia and I had a sandwich. The kids ordered the chicken and chips, expecting the usual breaded chicken strips or nuggets with fries. We had been shy of the fish and chips after being warned it would be nearly the entire fish served with the potatoes. So they thought the chicken and chips would be safe. They were sorely disappointed. Each of their plates had a roasted half-chicken sitting there, waiting to be picked apart. From then on nothing was ordered with chips.

We were done with Conwy, another town established to garrison a castle to subjugate rebels to English rule. Back on the motorway we skirted past Liverpool and Manchester. Rush hour traffic caught us in Bradford, but getting past Leeds was no problem. It wasn't long and a few roundabouts later we were off the main road and in York.

The York B&B reminded me of a large house in a college town that had been converted to use by students. A large dining room was just off the entry. At the end of the entry hallway was a stair leading up to rooms on either side of that hall. Our two rooms were downstairs. A quick trip through the kitchen took us to the back of the house where they were. They were connected, one right after the other, and shared one bathroom.

There was no time to rest. We were back on our feet and off for downtown, a walk of six blocks or more. The York Minster was the first stop. It is the largest medieval structure in the UK, begun in 1220 and finished in 1472. The large stained glass windows were most impressive. One was placed around 1260. Another is the world's largest area of medieval stained glass in a single window.

The original church had been hastily built with wood in the 7th century to perform the baptism of Edwin of Northumbria. He was king of Northumbria in the early 600's. Princess Ethelburga of Kent, a Christian, had married him and he was 'convinced' to convert. In a later century a Danish (Viking) king had also converted and was later buried in the York Minster. York was held by different groups from the 8th century to the 11th. Danes, Saxons, Norse, Scots, and Normans marauded back and forth. It still happens; American, Japanese, even French.

That was all fine, but two things were on our minds at the moment, the upcoming Ghost Walk of York we were planning on taking and food, but definitely not in that order. Following directions given to us by a sympathetic college student, we wandered down streets, passed through the Shambles, and finally came to our promised destination, the only US food outlet we visited in England, Pizza Hut. Ahh, but it was well worth it, probably the only thing that would have hit the spot right then. It was a large establishment, and it was packed. Pizza Hut was alive and doing well in York.

With satisfied stomachs we walked a few more blocks to the Ouse Bridge, over the Ouse River. Here, outside a pub, a group gathered to be led on a tour of sites with a gruesome, or at least intriguing history. York has the distinction of being known as the most haunted city in the UK. The guide for our group gave us many anecdotes and some humorous comments. As the group passed dark alleys and bar entrances, each with questionable smells and sights, prone and retching figures, I was thankful to be traveling with a safe number of people. In some ways the living denizens of York were more frightening to me.

One of the sights of the tour was Clifford's Tower, where a massacre of the Jewish community of York occurred in 1190. At that time the Christians were caught up in one of their many crusades to free the Holy Lands. Financing the crusades was a burden; many of the local officials were in debt. Jewish lenders serviced the debt; money lending was a sin for Christians. With the hopes of eliminating some lenders, and debts, a riot was stirred up against the Jews. They gathered and hid in Clifford's Tower. Leaving the tower meant either baptism or torturous death. Those inside torched the place in a mass suicide. Again we are reminded it is often the tragic that lives on in history.

That night, back at our B&B, it probably wasn't the stories from the ghost tour that made us all uneasy as we slept on the ground floor at the back of the house. It might have been the pizza, but most likely it was the pub-crawlers we saw while on the walk.

# DAY NINE: *Actual Poo*

Now it would be an appropriate, although likely unnecessary, time to confess my minimal grasp of the history of the British Isles. For so long to me the island and its inhabitants have been merely 'British'. The Scottish struggle for autonomy as depicted in the movie *Braveheart* and our drive through Wales revealed at least two groups of peoples that definitely did not consider themselves to be English. My recent research through multiple web sites and books has given me the beginning of a better understanding of what I am sure every student in England already knows.

Since the account of our morning in York and our drive to Corbridge will take only a few pages, this may be a good place to pass on some of what I have learned. I hope to keep it brief and accurate, but please bear with me.

Paleolithic man spread from wherever he originated to eventually inhabit all hospitable areas of the world. For the moment we will just consider the development of mankind in Europe. In the early stages governing or organization was very loose, maintained on a family or tribal level. As populations became stationary and increased government became inevitable. It was an important part of peace, war, and trade.

Modern anthropologists and historians use shared traits; such as language, technology, burial customs, and building characteristics, to identify related groups. One such group arose in central Europe and spread both east and west, eventually settling on the British Isles, too. Historians have labeled this group as the Celts. When they arrived the original Stone Age inhabitants of Britain were either annihilated or incorporated. So that at the time of the Roman arrival the tribes of the Celts were the native people of the land.

The recorded history of England begins with the invasion of the Roman armies. Although the early incursions were repulsed, Roman rule finally became effective for most of the island by 85 AD. Resistance from the Welsh and the Pictish tribes of the north continued. During the occupation of three centuries the tribes of central and southeastern England became a Romanized culture.

In the fourth century, due to threats nearer home, Roman troops were pulled back from the frontiers, including the British Isles. Within a few years the withdrawal was complete and the Romano-Britons were left to their own defenses. Almost immediately they were feeling pressure from the Picts and Scoti from the north and from Germanic tribes in the east and southern regions. It is thought that one of the early kings, Vortigern, hoped to settle the dilemma by inviting one of the tribes, the Saxons, to settle in return for aid against the Picts. The Saxons came, settled, and eventually ruled central and southern England. They spread as far west as the border with Wales. It was the connection with Wales that made the spread of Christianity possible among the Saxons.

It was at one of the religious centers that had been established, Lindesfarne, that Viking raiders first came ashore and began to spread their terror. From that date, 793 AD, for several centuries to come, the threat from the Danish raiders was a unifying force to all in England. Longboats even sailed up the Thames River and besieged London. Tribute was paid to get them to leave. Many of the Danish settled in the land. At one point, 1016 AD, a Danish king, Cnut, ruled over England. In 1042, Edward the Confessor wrested the rule back into English hands, but was continually harassed. It was this distraction, and internal intrigue, that facilitated the invasion from Normandy of William. It is only slightly ironic that the Normans themselves were descended from Vikings that a few centuries earlier had been given the northwestern lands of France to settle.

The Normans did not eliminate the Saxons, but they dominated them. Shortly after the death of William the Conqueror, Norman rule was complete over England and power was exerted over Wales, Ireland, and eventually Scotland. So it was by the 13<sup>th</sup> century that what we would recognize as England came to be.

The proper English inhabitant we see today has the roots of Celtic, Roman, Germanic, Scandinavian, and French influence. Perhaps that is the only way to explain how we get *Monty Python* and *Red Dwarf.*

◆    ◆    ◆

Back to the Full English for breakfast. By then it was only something to get over with in the mornings before we got on our feet for the day. Rick Steves had recommended getting to the Jorvik Viking Centre early in the morning to beat the queues. We were there before it opened and went right in. The first portion of the tour was a short film presentation on a brief history of the area.

The Romans had originally established a city there, Eboracum, in AD 71. In AD 306, Constantine the Great was made Emperor of Rome in Eboracum. The following century saw the withdrawal of Roman troops from England. This exodus left the Britons of Eboracum on their own. Initially that suited them quite well, until the Vikings came to town. Around 860AD it was more recognizable as a Viking trading center, then known as Jorvik.

Following the film introduction we boarded little carts for a thirteen-minute ride through the rest of the exhibit, a tour of the sights and smells of Jorvik, AD 975. After the ride was a walk-through of artifacts that had been unearthed in the area. The Centre seemed especially proud of the fossilized Viking 'poo' on display.

The final display before entering the gift shop was a man demonstrating how coins of the day were stamped. He explained the origination of the term 'sterling' for silver. The far off countries of the Middle East, the Easterlings, produced the best silver, Easterling silver. Kara got to take a whack at a blank coin to produce an image on it. From there it was a quick walk through the gift shop; they were all beginning to look the same. Exiting the building we saw the queues had indeed grown long, Rick does know a thing or two.

On our way back to the car we took one last pass through the Shambles and browsed a couple of shops there. The street there is very narrow, maybe four feet wide, with a three-foot sidewalk on either side. No cars could travel there, but I still couldn't help looking both directions before crossing. In earlier times it was the street of butchers' shops. The windows still had the wide bottom sill where the wares would be on display. One home of note along the Shambles was that of Margaret Clitherow. She was brought to justice in 1586 for hiding catholic priests and was condemned to death by pressing (crushing by a heavy weight). At times on our travels we were repelled by the barbaric methods employed to end life, but no doubt some future day our current societies will be viewed with the same distaste.

Back in our car we headed further north toward our next B&B in the small town of Corbridge, 2–3 hours away. After an uneventful drive we showed our ability once more to lose our way to our B&B. We passed the entrance and wound up in town. After filling the car with petrol we circled around the town center and were blocked by a crowd of people walking in the street. We crept slowly along behind what must have been a wedding party until we could turn off on a side street. Back on the main street we were quickly confronted by a large farm tractor. Someone in the car had just made some comment on the rural nature of the town and that we would probably run into some truck or tractor and then, sure enough, we did. I hugged the sidewalk with the car. Only minutes in town and we had already been to a riot and a tractor pull.

The B&B was like a 2-unit condo building; 2 stories, 3 bedrooms, 2 bathrooms, a kitchenette, and what we assumed was a clothes washer/dryer. We tried one load in it. It leaked a little and there was no drying. The downstairs bathroom had drying racks that we decorated with our one wet load and we left it at that. There was not much to see in the town that evening, so we vegged in front of the Telly. The shows weren't really interesting, but the commercials were entertainingly odd. A favorite of ours showed a man and woman sitting in front of their telly. She appeared distressed and their conversation went something like this.

Her— "You love football more than you love me."

Him, in an effort to soothe her— "What, playing or watching?"

# DAY TEN: On to Bonnie Scotland

According to legend, and film, the Greek armies laid siege to the city of Troy, eventually bringing it down to ruin. Trojan refugees then scattered by boat. One group sailed as far as the boot now known as Italy, pulling into a river to refresh water supplies. The women set fire to the boats because they did not want to travel any farther. Traveling with men will do that. It was at this site on the Tiber River that the settlement of Rome was started. By 400 BC the city was strong enough to be safe from local marauders. For the sake of homeland security the Roman defenders went out and conquered neighboring cities. They got so carried away they went on to conquer the local world powers of Carthage and Greece, becoming the rulers of the known world.

What place does a history of Rome have here? It has already been pointed out that most of England was ruled by Rome for most of the four centuries after AD 1. Some significant events of Roman history occurred on the British Isles. It was at York that Constantine was declared Emperor of Rome.

While researching I got lost in the descriptions of Emperor, Caesar, Augustus Prefect, and other titles for leaders of Rome. The essence is that shortly after becoming a separate identity, the Roman citizens wanted nothing to do with rule by a monarchy. The resulting government has been termed a republic. It wasn't a democracy, rule was by upper-class citizens, but it did succeed at preventing a monarchy. Although, at times a virtual monarchy was established when rule from a Caesar was passed on to offspring. Most often the ruler was determined by the Senate, but just as often it went to the most charismatic and victorious leader of one of the conquering armies away from the capital. The father of Constantine, Constantius, was one of the Caesars at the end of the third century AD. The Roman Empire had been divided into two portions, east and west, and ruled by two Caesars for the sake of efficiency. Constantius ruled the west and upon his death in 306 AD, the soldiers serving under him immediately declared his son, Constantine, as Augustus, a leveled-up Caesar. He returned to Rome to solidify his claim, eventually succeeding. It was Constantine that legalized Christianity and made it, in effect, the religion of Rome.

An interesting note to the York connection was the origin of the legion serving there. Legio IX had served Julius Caesar in Spain in 49 BC, earning much distinction, similar to the US 1$^{st}$ Cavalry. The legion had many recruits from Spain. One may ask if being sent to settle the hostile area around what is now York was to be considered a reward or a new challenge. Regardless, as a result there is undoubtedly Spanish blood in the current inhabitants of York, adding another ingredient to what makes up the modern British citizen. Just consider Manuel of *Fawlty Towers.*

◆     ◆     ◆

It was the last Full English; the next morning would be a Full Scottish. The start to every day was the same.

We had stopped in Corbridge because Hadrian's Wall was close. The wall had been built in the first century to mark the northern extent of Roman rule in Britain. Actually, Roman excursions had gone as far as the Scottish Highlands. But it seems the Highland clans were not at all tolerant of their presence. So, the Romans pulled back, built a wall, and posted 'Trespassers Will Be Crucified' signs.

The clans, tribes, the Romans were dealing with were initially known as the Caledonians. Not that they called themselves that, or Picts, or Scots, or Celts. There was no united nation, but rather a bunch of tribes who would at various times make war on each other or live in peace, just depending on the current mood. The presence of Roman troops gave them a reason to cooperate with each other to fight and harass the Romans, or else turn on each other and help the Romans. At some point the derogatory term used by the Romans, 'Picti—painted ones', stuck with them. About that same time a group from Ireland settled into the southwestern lands of Scotland. The locals referred to them as 'Scoti', meaning raiders. The two groups didn't form a union until around 843 AD, when they united to deal with another invader, the Viking.

Hadrian's Wall was built from the east coast to west coast of a narrow neck of Scotland. A second wall, the Antonine Wall, was built later around 140 AD, crossing at the more narrow neck from the sites of present-day Edinburgh to Glasgow. It was maintained for only a brief time before Roman troops were pulled back to the Hadrian. Life for the troops on this frontier was either particularly difficult or incredibly boring. Construction on the wall was considered a form of therapy, a means for keeping the mind and body busy, a group project. Idle time was not an option. One of the organizations for soldiers was known as the Cult of Disciplina. Sounds like a good name for a band.

The wall was built with Milecastles at regular intervals where 8–32 soldiers could be garrisoned. Later, forts were established where larger numbers of troops and regional officers could be housed. Several of the forts had rather odd names. Once Brewed National Park sounded like, well, a brewery. Brocolitia reminded me of a vegetable. Mons Grapius could have been the term for a body part, or a feature on the moon. The nearby fort we were going to visit was called Chester's Fort, a total lapse of imagination.

In preparing for our trip to England we had heard much in the news about the ravages of hoof and mouth disease that was afflicting a number of the cattle there. At that time the cows just had a foot in the mouth, later they got mad. Well, this was the only place in England where we had to take any precautions and this was merely a quick step into vats of disinfectant as we entered and exited the site. The remains of the fort were grouped in a large, grassy meadow. The stone remnants had been excavated by archeologists from the surrounding ground. It was mainly the foundations and underground structures that were available. The river associated with the site was respectably down the hill from the fort. As for the wall itself, the only standing portion was at most five feet above ground level. As Kara stood on it I had to squat down with the camera to give the idea of her being on top of Hadrian's Wall.

It was quite interesting to wander through what was left of the structures. The layout was so well planned and the buildings were constructed with such exactness. A number of the buildings were barracks for the soldiers, non-descript, box-like structures. One building was the residence of the commander. It was no more than a larger, box-like foundation. But instead of the stones of the floor being on the earth, it was shown how the stones for this building's floor were a foot or so off the ground. Steam or hot water could be sent under the floor for sub-floor heating. Nearer the river was a bathhouse with different rooms for the hot, cold, and mixed temperature baths. They tried to bring a little comfort and warmth to this dreary land.

We didn't stay for too long because we were a trifle chilled and Edinburgh was beckoning. We were eager to finish this last leg of our journey. After a short ways north we passed through the Cheviot Hills, the border with Scotland and England. The hills were heavily forested and at the top of the pass was a sign informing us we were entering Scotland. There is not much to recall of the passage from that point into Edinburgh. Our road did pass over the River Tweed, the earlier border. It turned out that as the road we were on continued into Edinburgh it became the road that our B&B was on. It was actually one block off the main road, but close enough. It was quite easy to locate.

We fell in love with the accommodations instantly. The home was newly remodeled on the inside. The plush carpets, high ceilings, roomy bedrooms, and delightful bathrooms were a joy to behold. To top it off, the host had us at ease right away with his Scottish accent. He informed us his wife, Grace, (Rick Steves referred to her as 'Amazing Grace') was out of town for the next day or so and that he would be seeing to things for us. We knew we were in for a fun time.

The first order of business was a quick trip to the TI (tourist information) centre downtown. Kara and Chris needed to send an email to significant ones back in the colonies. A plaid taxi answered our phone call and we zipped downtown. The rest of the time we were in Edinburgh we would be walking the 2–3 miles into town. A decent mall was located underneath the TI. We walked through but didn't linger long because we had purchased tickets for the double-decker tour bus and wanted to get a ride in before they quit for the day. We would be back to the mall to see some of the shops at a later time. I was especially drawn to the whisky shop at the bottom of the escalator. Oh yes, I would be back.

We hopped on the bus for only half of the tour. Disembarking at a location on the bus tour that was nearest to our route back to our B&B, we laid out the route we would take many times in the following days. The day was July 1st, Tim's birthday. We wandered a few streets off our main route and located a very nice Chinese restaurant. We were seated at a large table and the meals were placed on a large lazy susan in the middle. As a birthday present we didn't ask any staff to sing, or for any special hat for him to wear, or even for any special cake.

While winding down for the evening back at our B&B we had the telly on to catch the latest commercials. One channel was connected to a camera looking down on the entrance to the B&B. Not much was happening down there, but that put this channel on a level with several of the other stations available. Georgia and Kara were amused by a documentary delving into the lives of a polygamous "family" in Utah. We did not feel inclined to defend this part of life in America.

# DAY ELEVEN: A Pain in the Royal Mile

It is often amusing, and revealing, to see the appellations added to the names of those of ancient fame. Some were merely the addition of a title, such as Julius Caesar, Emperor Constantine, or Kings Henry I—VIII. Others were more descriptive and were used to either strike fear in their enemies or were comical to mock the owner. Examples would be Svein Forkbeard, Erik Bloodaxe, William the Conqueror, Edward the Confessor. The Scots had a different twist to the name thing. Robert the Bruce—just what is a 'bruce'? And the Black Knight or Green Knight I understand, but the Paisley Knight? Were there mediaeval Scottish hippies?

Since the departure of Roman garrisons the kings of England and Scotland have warred. There were intermittent periods of peace, mainly for the troops to rest. At the time of Robert the Bruce, the end of the 13th century, they were currently at peace. In 1272 AD, Edward Plantagenet was crowned King Edward I of England. He was itching to invade Scotland and it wasn't too long before the Scots gave him a reason. It had happened that in 1286, King Alexander III of Scotland died and left no heir to the throne except his granddaughter Margaret, daughter of the King of Norway. The arrangement was made for her to be wed to little Edward II of England. En route to the wedding she became ill and died. All at once thirteen Scottish nobles clamored for the title of King of Scotland. Being Scots, a lot of their clamoring was done with claymores, the famed Scottish sword. An appeal was made to Edward I to be an 'impartial' judge between the claimants, the strongest two being John Balliol and Robert the Bruce. Edward delayed making any judgment, knowing the bickering Scots would in the meanwhile tend to thin out some of the contenders on their own. When things got conveniently out of hand he insisted on stationing English garrisons in a number of Scottish castles on the pretense of restoring order. He even declared himself Lord Paramount of Scotland. Eventually Edward chose John Balliol mainly because he considered John more pliant to his English wishes. Under the terms set by Edward, King John was to answer to him and the people of Scotland were taxed to help pay for the current war England was having with France. Even Balliol couldn't stand for that and refused the terms, at the same time concluding a treaty with France himself for mutual aid. "Make my day," said Edward and his troops were quickly victorious. Scotland was his for the taking and he did that. Even the Stone of Scone, not only the first scone but also more importantly the sacred stone on which the Scottish kings received their crowns, was removed from the country and taken to Winchester for safekeeping. A number of rebels kept Edward busy for a few years until he finally silenced them.

During all these events the Bruce clan, and that was all a 'bruce' was, the family name altered from the Norman 'de Brus', had been waffling in loyalty between Scotland and England. Unfortunately the nobles of Scotland were often enough more motivated by personal gain and power than the overall good of the public. Finally the Bruce started to move away from English fealty and became a leader in the smoldering revolt. However, success was long in coming and he suffered defeat after defeat.

From that dismal period comes the myth of Bruce's spider. One day as the Bruce was in a cave, at the limit of his endurance, he sat watching a spider continually failing to spin its web and succeeding only after numerous attempts. It was a spiritual awakening, the Bruce felt encouraged to continue his struggle even as things continued to go against him. I really suspect some of that myth involved a certain Scottish medicinal brew. Anyway, he finally started winning and Edward decided to head north leading his army himself to nip the Bruce in the bud. By this time Edward was an old man, 50 at least, and died on the way. It then became the duty of Edward II and we all know from the movie what a pansy he was. He decided to wait a bit before making any rash moves. During this time the Bruce removed any competitors to the throne, in the typical Scottish way. He became recognized the ruler and eventually decided to invade England. Edward II was forced to respond and he led a large army north. At Bannockburn the heavily outnumbered Scottish army routed the English. A later second attempt by the English was also repulsed. Even though he was getting on in years himself, King the Bruce lived to witness a peace treaty signed in 1328 with King Edward III that recognized Scotland as an independent nation. He was actually a fairly much-admired ruler.

Now for the Paisley Knight. Paisley is nothing more than the name of a location, but guess what fabric pattern was developed there. Thanks to the movie *Braveheart*, there is a wealth of information on the life of William Wallace, the Paisley Knight. He was a real person and the screenplay may have gotten a few points correct. His father was killed by an English knight, but it was more likely when William was 20 years old, instead of 8. William had been shipped around to various relatives because of changing attitudes and allegiances among the Scottish nobles. It was that and his tendency to be a troublemaker. At one point he was in training for the priesthood, but that was terminated when he and some friends of his wound up killing a few English soldiers that had been harassing them. He switched careers from priest to outlaw. In his early years he was nothing more than a very troublesome brigand employing guerilla tactics against the disliked, occupying English forces. He did have a female acquaintance that was executed because she had assisted him in one of his escapes. Historians aren't clear on the nature of their relationship, but he did respond to her execution by slaughtering the local sheriff and garrison. This act leveled him up in lawlessness.

At the time there was no recognized rebellion going on, just hotspots here and there. And it is true, King Edward I was not a nice man. In one town on the border with Scotland, he had all the citizens of Berwick, 20,000 men, women, and children, brutally murdered because they had resisted his troops' entry into the town. It didn't help their plight any that the townsfolk had gathered on the walls and taunted him personally with insults and gestures. When word of his vengeful response was heard the clans rallied and united against him. A few high-placed noblemen joined with Wallace and with the aid of other clans they defeated an unarguably superior English force at Stirling. And yes, there really was an Irishman, named Stephen, a good friend and compatriot of Wallace. The following loss to the English at Falkirk dimmed the rebels' hopes. Although it makes for a very poignant scene, Robert the Bruce sitting with a bucket on his head and acting as a lackey for King Edward, record actually places the Bruce at his estate at the time of the battle, over one hundred miles away. Regardless, Wallace was captured by betrayal and suffered a very uncomfortable downsizing. Death by lethal injection was not in practice yet, though if it could be done very painfully I'm sure it would have been embraced by the executioner's profession. As it was, only the head of Wallace made it to London, to rest on a pike on the Tower Bridge. We had seen it earlier on while in the London Dungeon.

Just one more aside to the movie, the literature of the time makes it most probable that the Scots, though feisty and wiry, didn't paint their faces blue and flash their white arsses. That only happens in reality at modern rugby matches.

◆     ◆     ◆

That morning the Full English Breakfast was presented with another Scottish twist. Porridge, oatmeal, was offered as an option. The kids welcomed the change; life was getting better. I stuck with the full meal, pre-Atkins deal. We had already paid for it—dammit! Now that I think about it; that 'Full English Breakfast' that each B&B offered was a pretty good deal for them. How much skill can be required to fry up the various ingredients? Sure, they had to get up and throw something respectable together and I was very grateful for the sustenance. But it does tend to level the field for all of them. How can one reasonably expect a noticeably better, let alone different, Full English from one B&B to the next? The industry had a good deal going there.

Our first goal of the day was to drop off our rental car. This portion of the drive was far worse than the narrow roads in Wales. To get to the agency I had to drive through downtown Edinburgh. I was grateful the previous day's tour bus had taken us on a few of the same streets. Even though some of it was partially recognizable, we still wound up lost. There were too many one-way streets and angled intersections, and name changes. We drove around for far too long and I was bugged, more than mildly at that. Someone in a parking lot gave us directions, Georgia had asked, and at last we saw the sign to the agency, as we passed it. All was not lost, we were able to turn around, possibly not legally, and finally we were there. At last I could relax, the burden of driving in the UK was over. Better yet, the car still had its side mirrors, there were no scratches on it, and I hadn't come close to any pedestrians or autos, at least not while my eyes were open.

From the auto agency we trekked on foot toward Edinburgh Castle. From our approach it was perched on a rocky crag a hundred feet or so above us. Chris kidded about climbing the rocks up to the castle. Once we got inside the castle we were amused to learn that had been on of the more daring ways it had been captured once. However, this time our entrance was through the front gates. On either side of the gate was a statue of King Robert the Bruce on one and Sir William Wallace on the other. By the way, Wallace bore no resemblance to Mel Gibson whatsoever.

Once inside we were impressed that this was the most upkept castle of all we had seen, including the Tower of London. It had been used for military purposes up through WWII. We spent some time wandering through this castle. The attractions we browsed were: St. Margaret's chapel, the Dog Cemetery, the military prison, Mons Meg, and the Honours, or Royal Jewels of Scotland. I must say the Honours impressed me much more than the Crown Jewels in London. Still, a castle is a castle and we had finally had our fill.

We exited the castle and started our walk down the Royal Mile. The road down from the castle to Holyrood Palace is actually a little over a mile. It was the main avenue for tourists, as was evident from the number of shops along the way, and the fellows out playing pipes. After stepping into one or two of the shops we decided they were all the same. Diversions into the John Knox House and the Writer's Museum helped a bit. All in all, we were worn out before reaching the end of the mile. Near the end we wandered through an old cemetery before catching the tour bus for the ride home. On our way back to the B&B we found a Thai restaurant, feasted, and stumbled home. It had been a long day.

# DAY TWELVE: *The Spirit of Scotland*

Scotland–the home of bagpipes, kilts, haggis, Scotch whisky, and poets.

We are sitting together tonight in the fire glow,
Just you and I alone,
And the flickering light falls softly
On a beauty that's all your own.
It gleams where your round, smooth shoulder
From a graceful neck sweeps down;
And I would not exchange your beauty
For the best-dressed belle in town.

I have drawn the curtain closer,
And from my easy chair
I stretch my hands toward you,
Just to feel that you are there.
And your breath is laden with perfume,
As my thoughts around you twine,
And I feel my pulses beating
As your spirit is mingled with mine.

And the woes of this world have vanished
When I've pressed my lips to yours;
And to feel your life-blood flowing
To me is the best of cures.
You have given me inspiration

For many a soulful rhyme-
You're the finest old Scotch whisky
I've had for a long, long time.
Author Unknown (but evidently sufficiently inebriated)

The ancient Egyptians employed distillation, as did the Chinese, Greeks, and Romans. However, the liquids they produced were used most often as solvents and unguents instead of drink. That was the domain of ales and beers. Irish monks of the 5th century, in particular St. Patrick, the father of all Irish monks, figuratively, traveled the European continent in their labors and were there exposed to the spirit of distillation. Supposedly it was St. Patrick who brought the knowledge of the process back to Ireland and when he was not tormenting snakes, druids, or converts he was distilling *usque baugh,* Irish Gaelic for 'the water of life'. It was known as 'the water of life' because it had been noted that dead tissue would be preserved when immersed in it. There must have always been a fascination with sticking things in alcohol. The name 'whisky' is a result of the English mispronunciation of *uisque braugh,* the Scots Gaelic for it.

Early on whisky was a product of home distilleries and was used as a medicinal tonic. It was taken three times daily to ward off disease and even breakfast was preceded by a wee dram. A dram was no specific measure, depending solely on the generosity of the pourer.

As it is with any good medicine and government, the English government made many attempts at regulating the production of whisky immediately after Scotland signed the Act of Union with England in 1707. It wasn't so much the control of production as it was the potential revenue from the sales tax that was desired. As result, many of the easy targets, large distilleries, were driven out of business. The illicit home-brewers could more easily avoid detection and made a good business with smuggling the whisky, which was of a better quality even. As a side note, when our government attempted the prohibition of alcohol, then obtainable only through a doctor for 'medical' purposes, whisky was smuggled into the country. One of the most reputable suppliers was Captain Bill McCoy, hence the term 'the real McCoy'.

Although currently some acceptable amount of taxation has been reached, whisky taxes have remained high in Europe: UK-67%, France-56%, Greece-42%, and Spain-37%. The auctioneer Christie's sold one bottle of aged, single malt for 6,374 pounds. Imagine the tax on that.

Considering that 1½-ounce of Scotch whisky contains only 104 calories and with its reputed (?) medicinal qualities, give me a wee dram of Macallan in the morning and I'll be ready for my Full English Breakfast.

◆    ◆    ◆

Breakfast; full English or full Scottish, they were all the same, but only two more to go. Afterward we hoofed it downtown and caught a tour bus. The guide made a point of asking passengers where they were from. It wasn't merely for the sake of being friendly, for he was; rather it was that he wanted to get a jab in at every nationality present. He was better than a Disney guide; note to Disney, the bottle by his seat surely helped. On the bus we toured out from Edinburgh to Leith, the port where the Royal Yacht *Britannia* is moored.

The *Britannia*, you can take it or leave it. Now Leith is interesting. Traditionally Leith was the port access for Edinburgh. The two cities were separate until the sprawl of 'Auld Reeky' joined the two. In a classic case of democracy in action, Leith was merged with Edinburgh in 1920 after the people of Leith had voted five to one against it. The earliest record of golf is connected with Leith. King James II banned it in 1457 because it interfered with the more practical sport of archery. More recently, Irvine Welsh, author of *Trainspotting* was born there. And computer game developers Rockstar North, responsible for *Grand Theft Auto*, are based there.

Our first destination after the bus ride was the Dynamic Earth, a science-center-like affair. The kids and I spent a few hours wandering through it. Once you went through the door for the tour there was no turning back until you reached the end. Besides, there was a little café in the building. While we had done the tour, Georgia had walked down the street to Holyrood Palace and had an enjoyable time herself. Her time was probably more peaceful as she didn't have groups of school kids milling around her.

The Dynamic Earth happened to be the starting place for our next adventure. One half mile from there was the approach to Arthur's Seat, a low mountain rising up on the southeast of town. History had it that the summit was the site of the king's coronation in ancient times. The hike up was quite brisk. We were fooled by what we thought was the beginning of the ascent; it merely took us around the side of the crag to where a parking lot marked the actual trailhead. But in doing so we had hiked along the very rock crag where James Hutton (1726–1797) was inspired to develop his new theory of geology, that rock and earth formations tell the story of the ancient earth. He also had some thoughts about natural selection and it was his book that Charles Darwin enjoyed while sailing on the *Beagle*.

The origin of the name for the mountaintop, Arthur's Seat, is not too clear. Most have assumed it was connected with the legends of King Arthur. Although the current tales locate the round table down in Wales or southwestern England, it is thought the early stories originated in Scotland. At least that is what many Scots will say. And they will probably even claim to have discovered America and the Internet.

In medieval times Castle Edinburgh was known as 'the Castle of Women'. Many of the stories have female prisoners held there. A different version has Morgan la Fay, of the King Arthur tale, as the ruler in the castle. Then in some others the castle is populated by seductive women seeking to lure knights from their holy errands. Consider Pure Sir Lancelot in Monty Python's *Quest for the Holy Grail.* Finally, other historians claim the name, Arthur's Seat, is merely a corruption of

'Archer's Seat', the original designation. But what do you think people really want to remember it as?

No matter what the history of the rock is, thousands of people make the hike to the top each year. Once on the top we had to find our own patch of rock to rest on, a small crowd was already present. We asked a young fellow to snap a picture of all of us there. In the ensuing conversation we learned he was an American attending a university in England. Going back down we took a different route and veered off the main path to explore some ruins we saw. It was St. Anthony's chapel, used by monks centuries ago mainly to watch for ships entering the Firth of Forth. It was after the Viking days, so they would not run and hide from approaching vessels, but would run down and collect duties or fees from them, holy Vikings. Evidently they had some sort of tax on ships that entered the port. It must have been God's port and he expected his dues.

After exploring around there for a bit we continued on down. A major street runs along the foot of the hill. Across that street is a large football field and next to that is Holyrood Palace. Coming down we could see cars being parked on the sports field next to the palace. Some sort of official 'tea party' was going on. Women with large hats and men dressed in kilt and suit jacket were getting out of the cars and entering the palace. All were in formal wear and I was impressed with the look. For us to pass the area we had to stay on the other side of the street with the other commoners.

Back on the Mile we went to the Tron, not a sci-fi character, an old church on the street corner. There we booked a tour of the local underground and learned of Edinburgh's dark moments and early lifestyles. After the guide's explanation, the phrase 'gardee loo' took on a whole new meaning. That would be the only warning a person walking along on the street would get as a pot load of wastes would be tossed out of a window above. The tour wasn't as enjoyable as the York Ghost Walk, but it was fun enough, especially in this age of flushing toilets.

While we were waiting for the tour we had a minor treat. We had stepped outside the church to wander around while waiting. A group of cars, led by motorcycle police, was making its way down the street. I thought I was joking to the kids when I said something to the effect of, "Here comes the Queen." Sure enough, as one car passed just feet from us we could see a nice little old lady sitting in the back seat and occasionally waving to people outside. It was only the Queen Mother herself. I have been blessed by royalty.

There were only two important stops to make before returning for the night. Tim had found a Games Workshop on the mile and he had to purchase a few Warhammer figures before we left. Then I had to return to the mall we had discovered the first day in town. I had told the whisky shop I would return. There I learned whisky is not just whisky. Scotland is divided into five different regions where the spirit produced there is each unique and distinctive from the others. This is due to the differences in the peat used for the fires, the water, and the grains. I had a brief lesson on blends, single malts, and aging times. I made my own purchase and had my own war hammer to bring home.

# DAY THIRTEEN: *Cheers*

This was to be our last full day in the United Kingdom. I have nothing more to say about breakfast, other than the reason we would be leaving with heavy hearts was largely due to twelve mornings of ingesting a Full English Breakfast. Little did we know that our views of breakfast would be forever altered. However, as a parting treat to ourselves we did have dinner reservations at Cirro's that evening. More on that later.

This was the day to catch the art gallery and museums we had so far missed. We did not want to repeat our mistake with the British Museum in London where we had allowed ourselves only two hours to see the place. We wanted plenty of time, maybe too much time. Finally, the rain threatened to hamper us for this day. So far the weather had been mostly clement, much better than we had anticipated. It was just as well we had planned to be inside for most of the time. We could wander freely in large buildings all day.

The National Gallery was the first stop. The collection of artwork was truly amazing. It was something to see the large paintings and imagine all the work that went into creating each. And then to see the dates on some of them. There were levels and wings of paintings, paintings, and more paintings. It was actually quite tiring. We tried to be faithful to seeing everything there was to see, but we were all eager to walk through the exhibit. We had a well-deserved quick lunch before the next marathon.

The Museum of Scotland and the Royal Museum were a joined building; so one stop took care of these two. Again it was the displays of ancient Scottish history that were the most interesting. The more recent the time period shown in the display, the more quickly we moved on through. Then really, how many significant pebbles and artifacts can one stand to stare at after all? This day was possibly one of the most tiring because of all the standing and staring at small objects, not to mention all the hanging artwork. We were done seeing the sights on our trip.

To top off our day, and our time in Edinburgh, we were anticipating an evening at Cirro's, a restaurant our B&B host had recommended upon our arrival. Several times we had walked past the place on our way back from downtown sightseeing. Each time it had been closed. We weren't able to see inside through the door window. And since it was only one of several shops in a large, rather plain building, we didn't know what to expect of the place.

We hurried back to our B&B to freshen up before going out for the evening. Then we dropped our bags of souvenirs and pamphlets and headed out the door. We had walked less than a block when our host, also a cab driver, pulled alongside us and wanted to give us a ride down to Cirro's. The day was July 4th, and he wanted to treat us in honor of the 4th. Really nice folks over there. I do wonder if an Englishman would have been as pleased to treat us on the 4th as a Scotsman was.

After entering through the small front door it was apparent the interior was hardly any more of a presentation than the outside. It was small, cozy they would call it, but nice. There were maybe six tables inside and we took the largest one. Our waiter for the evening then came and welcomed us. Dressed in dark slacks and tie, white shirt and serving apron, he was a very nice, older gentleman with such a soothing demeanor. This was a family business. The daughter was the world-trained chef, the mother and father provided service.

Having a four-course meal was a novelty in itself, but each course was so excellently prepared and presented that the whole experience was a treat. Our server patiently led us through our selections. For the first course there were various seafood selections available: shrimp, fried squid, and battered mussels. We all shared a couple of servings of cheesy bread sticks. We next had the choice of various salads and soups. Georgia had a vegetable soup while the rest of us had salads. The kids decided salads were easier to pick through than soups. For the main course Georgia had the dinner salad, I had a poached Scottish salmon, Chris tried a beef dish, Kara dared the lamb again, and Tim settled for the chicken. Everyone seemed pleased with their choice. I had a coffee for dessert and shared a pastry with Georgia. The kids each had their own dessert dish. We all agreed that we had had enough and that it was all prepared and served so exquisitely.

When the B&B host had told us that Cirro's served fine Scottish food, the servings weren't really what we had originally expected, thank goodness.

The only authentic Scottish food we could think of was haggis. As it turned out, haggis wasn't even on the menu. None of us even had to consider it as a choice.

In these days I would bet that even few Scots have tasted a haggis. It is definitely not a staple, probably most often associated with the week commemorating the work of the Scottish poet, Robert Burns. Groups will gather and sit solemnly as a tray carrying the gastronomical aberration is carried in while a bagpipe plays. After quoting a line or two of Burns, the master of ceremonies plunges a knife into the mound and everyone digs in. It sounds almost like some kind of religious experience. I confess that it would require the presence of more than one dram of spirits to put me in the proper frame of mind to partake.

So what is a haggis? It is a mixture of ground organs (heart, liver, and kidneys), plus suet, onions, and oats. This mixture is placed inside a sheep's stomach and cooked. These days it can be purchased in cans instead of stomachs, haggis light. Evidently grocers have had a difficult time stacking stomachs on shelves. Obviously not the choice parts of the lamb, it was more than likely symbolic of what was left to the Scottish folk once the occupying army had extracted what they considered were their proper dues. Now it is more of a novelty, much the same as the century egg and rocky mountain oysters. More are probably foisted on tourists than the locals.

As we exited Cirro's and walked the few blocks back to our B&B we each realized the trip was over, virtually. We would try to cram our essentials and souvenirs into our bags and settle in for a final sleep in the motherland. And the next morning we could even skip breakfast.

◆        ◆        ◆

There wasn't much to report on the exit from England. Our host was our ride to the airport. Our carry-on bags had been stuffed to capacity and we had been stuffed in a like manner into the taxi. It was a testy little drive to the airport and I was sure glad it was someone else driving.

We had a brief wait at the airport. We just sat, this was one place we were not obligated to explore. Exchanging the last of our UK currency was all we attempted. Before long we were on a KLM plane bound for Amsterdam, where we breathed Dutch air, changed planes, and flew straight to Seattle.

We were all happy to return home. I felt that I had come back a little different person. I had seen, heard, smelled, tasted, and experienced another part of the world. My life had been enriched in ways that couldn't have happened otherwise. Accomplishing this with my family was central to the extreme pleasure of the experience. To this day I feel those two weeks were undeniably some of the best days of my life.

Unlike my vacation trip experiences as a child, this time I was happy to be returning home. We all had familiar people, surroundings, and routines that we had missed. I enjoy my place in the world. I love the weather and the scenery of where we live in western Washington. I am comfortable with my work and with the community we live in. I knew I could come home and relax from the enjoyable, but really hectic, sightseeing tour of England. Definitely a time of settling down was needed.

As a child I had always counted on bringing back a souvenir from the places I had visited, something to serve as a reminder I had experienced another space in this world. On this trip, other than the fine Scotch whisky, I was only bringing home memories. These would possibly be more meaningful and lasting than any small object I could bring back. Perhaps, like the Scotch, they will age well to perfection. I am still discovering flavors and nuances from them.

Admittedly I had begun this treatise with an exploration of the Full English Breakfast. It was, after all, the sole British food offering that was promised at the beginning of the trip. But there was so much more to take in. We sampled international foods as well as local offerings. We had breathed the air, smelled the smells, and heard the sounds of life of the city of London and the countryside of Tintern Abbey. We saw and touched stones that had been hewn by human hands one thousand, even two thousand years ago. We felt the attitudes and spirit of various locales. We had all experienced another part of the world, expanding our vision of our world.

Above all, preeminent to the extreme pleasure I derived from the trip was that we had done it as a family. We left home and returned together. We endured the long flights and harrowing drives. We walked the many miles of streets, longed for timely meals, and slept in a number of B&Bs. We tromped through castles, cathedrals, and up Arthur's Seat. This time together was never a source of friction or an obligation to endure one another. Instead, it amplified the whole experience. We each had five sets of senses to use each day for discovery. How I loved, then as now, exploring the world with my family.

After we had walked through the door of our home, been welcomed by the cats, and put away some of our stuff, I sat at my desk to reflect on what I had felt through it all. I was quickly overcome by a deep sensation of total happiness, satisfaction, and fulfillment. I felt such a pleasurable joy that I was aware that I could gladly accept death at that moment. I had just lived two of the best weeks of my life. Not that I wanted to die right then, I fervently hoped to feel such fulfillment many more times. But at that very moment I was a very happy man.

Georgia, my love, Kara, Chris, Tim…. I thank each of you for that marvelous time. It was nothing more than you being yourselves, and me, too, and all of us being together that made that experience. May we all have more such moments in our lives.

978-0-595-47803-3
0-595-47803-4